INVITATION TO A

LAVISH
FEAST

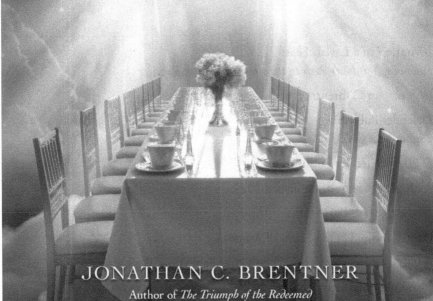

INVITATION TO A
LAVISH
FEAST

Following Wisdom's Path to the Pre-Tribulation Rapture

JONATHAN C. BRENTNER

Author of *The Triumph of the Redeemed*

DEFENDER
CRANE, MO

Invitation to a Lavish Feast
Following Wisdom's Path to the Pre-Tribulation Rapture

by Jonathan C. Brentner

Defender Publishing
Crane, MO 65633

© 2025 Defender Publishing

All Rights Reserved. Published 2022

ISBN: 978-1-948014-89-2

Printed in the United States of America.

A CIP catalog record of this book is available from the Library of Congress.

Cover designer: Jeffrey Mardis
Interior designer: Katherine Lloyd

To my wonderful wife, Ruth:
for her amazing kindness, loving support,
and encouragement, without which this book
would not have been possible.

CONTENTS

ACKNOWLEDGMENTS

To Terry James, my brother in the Lord and dear friend, for his ongoing encouragement, guidance, and support in my ministry.

Angie Peters, for her hard work in editing this book.

Bruce Duell, for his friendship and encouragement during the many difficult times of my life.

My professors at Talbot Theological Seminary who provided a firm foundation of learning in the mid-1970s that has lasted up to this moment:

Dr. Charles Fienberg
Dr. Robert Thomas
Dr. Richard Rigsby
Dr. Henry Holloman
Dr. Robert Saucy

THE PATH
OF BIBLICAL WISDOM

A Christian theology of wisdom begins and ends with Christ. The New Testament identifies Jesus as the ultimate source of wisdom. The Old Testament anticipated an eschatological fulfilment of wisdom, both by its call to wisdom as well as by Israel's failure to live by that wisdom. In Christ Old Testament motifs related to wisdom found their fulfilment and reconfiguration. Old Testament wisdom was revelatory, organizing life around the fear of the Lord. In the New Testament this life is reoriented around Christ's invitation to the wisdom of the gospel.[1]

—Daniel J. Ebert IV, *The Wisdom of God*

My journey toward writing this book began one Sunday when an associate pastor at the church my wife and I attended said something that instantly struck me as wrong. Among the several hundred who had heard His words that morning, I suspect very few sensed anything terribly amiss with his statement.

I checked the recording of each of the three services that day to confirm what I had heard: "The completion of our redemption happens at the appearing of the New Jerusalem." I already knew he denied the existence of such events as the Rapture, the seven-year Tribulation, and a literal thousand-year reign of Jesus over the nations, but why did he zoom past Jesus' Second Coming and point to the start of eternity as the completion of our salvation?

In the weeks that followed, I began to understand how making the appearance of the New Jerusalem the centerpiece of our hope dismisses Jesus' preeminent place in the end times. He is our expectation of glory; our hope does not rest in a far-distant event with no relevance to our daily lives. He is the focal point of our "blessed hope;" our expectation doesn't rest in an event long after our death, but rather in Jesus' glorious appearing!

Notice the Apostle Paul's words in the verses below:

> But our citizenship is in heaven, and from it we await a Savior, the Lord Jesus Christ, who will transform our lowly body to be like his glorious body, by the power that enables him even to subject all things to himself. (Philippians 3:20–21)

Bible prophecy points our hearts to the Savior. The anticipation of His imminent return is the substance of all that we long for. Because of His promises, we can step out of bed in the morning to face a world fraught with danger and an enemy who continually plots to discourage our hearts with repeated attacks.

In light of these truths, how can we possibly regard what Scripture teaches about the end times as tertiary, or as being less important than other matters having to do with our faith? No, no, no! The "blessed hope" of the gospel (Titus 2:11–14) is the Rapture, when Jesus gives us immortal bodies and takes us to Heaven to the place He's preparing for us. Those who take the focus of our hope away from the Savior greatly err.

I didn't leave the service that morning thinking I would write another book; that decision didn't happen until much later. In the months that followed, however, I began to see that the associate pastor's words not only contradicted God's Word, but they also made an event, rather than Christ, the epicenter of attention. Soon I again felt the passion swelling inside me to defend what the Bible says about our hope, but this time from a different perspective.

Jesus' Preeminence

My thoughts concerning what I heard that Sunday morning first led to a deeper insight regarding what Paul wrote about Jesus' preeminence in

Colossians 1:15–20. Considering the grandness of the following words the apostle wrote concerning our Lord, shouldn't we also expect Him to have a supreme and dominant role in what lies ahead?

> He is the image of the invisible God, the firstborn of all creation. For by him all things were created, in heaven and on earth, visible and invisible, whether thrones or dominions or rulers or authorities—all things were created through him and for him. And he is before all things, and in him all things hold together. And he is the head of the body, the church. He is the beginning, the firstborn from the dead, that in everything he might be preeminent. For in him all the fullness of God was pleased to dwell, and through him to reconcile to himself all things, whether on earth or in heaven, making peace by the blood of his cross.

Our belief that the Rapture can happen at any moment exalts Jesus as the object of our hope. More than that, it signifies to the world that He must be the One in charge of all that happens next. And that's exactly what the book of Revelation tells us. For not only is He the Head of the Church, but He's also the One who will ultimately judge the world, destroy the kingdom of the beast, return in great glory, and establish His thousand-year reign over the nations of the earth. Isn't that the heart of what it means for Jesus to be preeminent in all things? The descriptions of His grandeur and dazzling power all through the last book of the Bible stretch the imagination to its limit.

Consider the emphasis of Colossians 3:4: "When Christ who is your life appears, then you also will appear with him in glory." In this much-overlooked verse about the Rapture, the focus is Christ. He is our "life," and when He "appears," we "will appear with him in glory." The Greek word for "appear" is *phaneroo*, or to "reveal." It signifies an unveiling of what was previously hidden or unknown. It's the time when we will not only see Jesus in all His glory, but it's also the time when the Lord will unveil our true nature as redeemed saints.

John described the Rapture in a comparable way:

Beloved, we are God's children now, and what we will be has not yet appeared; but we know that when he appears we shall be like him, because we shall see him as he is. And everyone who thus hopes in him purifies himself as he is pure. (1 John 3:2–3)

Diminishing Jesus' Supremacy

The three most popular views of Bible prophecy significantly diminish the Bible's portrayal of Jesus' future magnificence. A key complaint I have is how each one negates the Lord's centrality in future events pertaining to us and the world. Not only that, but in most instances, these teachings make the Church—rather than our Savior—the key player in what lies ahead.

Replacement Theology is the belief that when the people of Israel rejected their Messiah, God turned His back on them and replaced the nation with the Church, which then became the recipient of His kingdom promises, albeit spiritually. Proponents of this view tell us there is no future Tribulation or thousand-year reign of Jesus. They identify the Church Age as Christ's rule over the nations, with the next event being Jesus' end-of-the-age return to inaugurate the eternal state.

Jesus' Second Coming thus becomes a matter-of-fact event rather than the visible and dazzling display of His magnificence and power that we read about in Revelation 19:16–20:4. The Apostle John's depiction of our Lord's glorious return to earth, taken as the apostle intended for us to understand it, aligns far closer with the words of Paul in Colossians 1:15–20 than with the words of those who tell us this event has already happened or that what we see today is the reality of what it means for Him to rule over the earth in the way described in Revelation 20:1–10.

The most popular teaching regarding the end times in today's churches is Dominion Theology. Its proponents teach that the Church will overcome today's rampant wickedness and lawlessness and reign over the nations *before* Jesus returns to the earth. Christians, not the Lord, will initiate the long-awaited Millennium.

This errant teaching not only makes the Lord's Second Coming essentially a non-event, but it also strips it of the magnificence so evident in its many biblical descriptions. Not only that, but this viewpoint exalts the Church over its Head, Christ; in so doing, it almost totally negates what Paul wrote about our Savior in Colossians 1:15–20.

Preterism, which teaches that Jesus returned to the earth in AD 70, also unduly exalts the Church and dulls the splendor and wonder of Scripture's description of His Second Coming. This viewpoint changes the wonder of Jesus' return as described in Revelation 19:11–20:4 into a nondescript event in the sky during the Roman siege of Jerusalem in the first century AD. With no Rapture or Second Coming in our future, our walk with the Lord during this lifetime becomes a hope in and of itself.

Where is the hope for suffering saints if all, or most, of the Lord's promises for our future reached their fulfillment almost two thousand years ago? It's grievously lacking. The belief of some preterists that Jesus will give us resurrected and immortal bodies at the end of the age helps, but this expectation also falls far short of what the Bible reveals about our hope as New Testament saints.

Premillennialism, on the other hand, maintains Jesus' exalted position with its literal interpretation of prophecy, including the prophecy given in the book of Revelation. This is the teaching that Jesus will return to the earth after a seven-year time of Tribulation on the earth, establish His kingdom, and rule for a thousand years. Premillennialists believe His kingdom will include a restored Israel, with Christ ruling from Jerusalem. This is the viewpoint I will defend in this book.

The New Testament points to Jesus as the substance of our hope. It tells us we will experience the fullness of our redemption when He appears (Romans 8:23–25; 1 Corinthians 15:51–55). We magnify His Name the most when we long for the time when we will meet Him in the air (1 Thessalonians 4:17; Philippians 3:20–21).

Jesus Personifies Biblical Wisdom

Exalting Jesus' place in Bible prophecy happens when we treasure the words of the One who said, "Heaven and earth will pass away, but my words will not pass away" (Matthew 24:35). Biblical wisdom not only lauds Jesus as the hub of all end-time events, but it also extols Him as the embodiment of truth.

Jesus, as the personification of biblical wisdom throughout the book of Proverbs, reveals His plans for the ages in the *words* He inspired for us on the pages of our Bibles. We see the close connection between the Savior and His words throughout the entire Scripture. In fact, John began His Gospel by referring to Christ as "the Word" (John 1:1).

Jesus' link between Himself and His words is especially prominent in Mark 8:38:

> For whoever is ashamed of me and of my words in this adulterous and sinful generation, of him will the Son of Man also be ashamed when he comes in the glory of his Father with the holy angels.

In the above warning, Jesus doesn't separate His words from His person. We find this theme repeated in the verses below:

> [Jesus said,] "Truly, truly, I say to you, whoever hears my word and believes him who sent me has eternal life. He does not come into judgment, but has passed from death to life." (John 5:24)

> So Jesus said to the Jews who had believed him, "If you abide in my word, you are truly my disciples." (John 8:31)

> Jesus answered him, "If anyone loves me, he will keep my word, and my Father will love him, and we will come to him and make our home with him." (John 14:23)

In His captivating description of Jesus' return to earth in the book of Revelation, the Apostle John noted that "the name by which he is called is The Word of God" (Revelation 19:13). He is the personification of God's revelation to humanity, the capstone of wisdom. Those who equate the Holy Spirit-inspired words of Revelation 19:11–20:4 with anything but Christ's future return and the establishment of His rule err greatly.

Words. They're key to the path of wisdom in all that we believe about the faith. Apart from words, we have no way to objectively evaluate the beliefs of others. When it comes to Bible prophecy, what we believe must align with the biblical text. Apart from what the words of Scripture tell us about what lies ahead for both us and the world, everything else is guesswork based on human intuition.

God's Character

After I began writing this book, a third way to discern the path of wisdom emerged. Not only must what we believe about future things align with the words of Scripture and exalt our Lord Jesus, but our beliefs must also align with God's character as revealed throughout the Bible.

In Ezekiel 36:22–23, we read that God bases His resolve to restore a kingdom to Israel on the necessity to "vindicate the holiness of my great name." This is just one example of how what we believe about the future of Israel must align with what the Bible reveals of God's character. We will see that this not only relates to our premillennial beliefs, but also to our trust in Jesus regarding salvation and the certainty of our hope.

One of the great passages in the New Testament concerning our salvation is Ephesians 2:1–10, in which Paul exalts the Savior as our only hope for the forgiveness of our sins and hope of eternal life. The apostle also notes how the grandeur of our deliverance aligns with God's character: "But God, being rich in mercy, because of the great love with which he loved us" (Ephesians 2:4).

Notice the emphasis regarding how our belief that Jesus saves us solely "by grace" and "through faith" lines up with the Father's characteristics of "mercy" and "great love." Wouldn't we expect the same to be true about our understanding of future things?

In chapter 11, we will examine the way Paul uses the restoration of a kingdom for Israel as an illustration of the security we enjoy in Christ. He connects both to God's "mercy," which then leads to His admonitions beginning in Romans 12.

Our "knowledge of the Holy One" provides us with a third assessment as to whether or not we have answered Wisdom's call and are traveling down its path.

Wisdom's Call

For decades, I've been in the habit of reading a chapter a day from the book of Proverbs, with each reading correlating to the day of the month. Slowly I've realized how Wisdom's call also relates to what we believe about future things.

Biblical wisdom doesn't represent a fourth test of the validity of such views, but it rather unites the streams of Jesus' preeminence, the words of Scripture, and God's character into one river. Wisdom calls us to a greater understanding of these matters, and in so doing, confirms our anticipation of Jesus' imminent appearing.

I know that is a rather bold claim, but the purpose of this book is to show how biblical wisdom verifies this anticipation.

My study of the Proverbs has led me to conclude that the personification of Jesus Himself—Wisdom—invites us to a lavish feast, one that will culminate in the marriage supper of the Lamb. Until then, our journey through this life at times will at times lead to much suffering, loss, and rejection. Some believers will face terrible persecution and even death because of their faith.

What, then, is so extravagant about the banquet to which Wisdom beckons us? It's all about the glories that lie ahead for us and how these eternal wonders bring us joy and help carry us through dark times. For example, I often wonder how I survived my past, which I can only refer to as "tumultuous." The only reason I was able to overcome those challenges is the biblical truth regarding Jesus' appearing and the hope it offers of a much better day to come.

Of course, the time of great jubilation in Heaven awaits us, but our anticipation of this glorious celebration brightens our days now—even in the midst of great sorrow. My passion to write about the doctrine of Jesus' imminent appearing is far more than just a matter of defending Jesus' preeminence in all things. *A biblical understanding of what lies ahead is the best preparation we can have for the many losses that will come our way in this life and for the chaos we might need to endure between now and when Jesus appears to take us home.*

Regardless of our circumstances, the Lord's steadfast love invites us to feast upon the abundance of His grace that will one day lead to our experience of everlasting life, along with its many delights.

> How precious is your steadfast love, O God!
> The children of mankind take refuge in the shadow of your wings.
> They feast on the abundance of your house,
> and you give them drink from the river of your delights.
> For with you is the fountain of life;
> in your light do we see light. (Psalm 36:7–9)

My prayer is that as you read this book, your insight into what Scripture reveals about the future will grow as you understand the vital link between the wisdom Jesus imparts to us regarding the end times and our hope of His imminent appearing to take us home to glory.

Section One

Wisdom's Defense
of Bible Prophecy

Today, Bible prophecy is under siege. There are atheists, secular humanists, liberal Christian theologians, posttribulationists, midtribulationists, preterists, and many others who are launching vitriolic attacks, particularly against pretribulationism.[2]

—Ron Rhodes, *Bible Prophecy under Siege*

Bible prophecy attracts much abuse from believers as well as from those who don't believe in Christ for salvation. Advocates of a pre-Tribulation Rapture in particular have become the brunt of much ridicule. Even many pastors of churches whose statements of faith claim belief in the inspiration and inerrancy of Scripture have joined the chorus of those mocking the expectation of Jesus' soon appearing.

How does wisdom fit into this picture? Am I really saying the book of Proverbs defends such matters as Jesus' millennial rule or His removal of the Church before the judgments begin, as recorded in Revelation chapters 6–18? Not exactly, but decades of reading a chapter a day from this book of wisdom has led me to conclude:

The more we understand about Jesus as Wisdom personified, the more we recognize the necessity of His millennial rule, and with it, a greater understanding of why we must meet Jesus in the air (1 Thessalonians 4:13–17) before the Day of the Lord judgments sweep over the planet.

This might seem extreme to some, but please know I don't make such an assertion based on my own insight or knowledge. As I will seek to demonstrate in this section, as well as in the remainder of this book, my conclusion arises solely from the *words* of Scripture. Isn't this what we do in other matters of belief? Isn't the text of the New Testament the foundation for our assurance that God has forgiven all our sins? Wisdom points us to words, which become the basis of what we believe and shape our expectation of Paradise.

When those outside the faith attack our arrogance for claiming to know the "truth" about the gospel, how do we respond? We point them to Jesus and His words. In doing so, we move the focus away from ourselves and directly toward what the Bible says. The hope of eternal life doesn't spring from our own wisdom. We don't base our security on what we know about life or our behavior (definitely not!), but *solely* upon the words of Scripture.

Many in the world criticize our "pride" for asserting that Jesus is the only path to eternal life. They see it as haughtiness that we'd even make such a statement. Isn't our response in such cases to point them to Jesus and His words in John 14:6— "I am the way, the truth, and the life. No one comes to the Father except through me"?

We didn't originate the idea of making Jesus the only way to Heaven; we believe it because that's what our Risen Lord said.

In the same way, my claim that biblical wisdom provides us with the first line of defense against those who mock our hope springs from a diligent study of the *words* of Scripture over six decades. It's definitely not anything that came via my own insight or limited knowledge, but rather from an understanding of God's Word.

Here is a summary of what God has taught me over the years regarding this matter:

When we apply the same historical-grammatical method of biblical inter-pretation to Bible prophecy as we do for the passages concerning Jesus' person, His claims, and the basics of the gospel we hold dear, we're led not only to a belief in Israel's future restoration as a nation, but also to an expectation of Jesus' imminent appearing.

What is the historical-grammatical method of biblical interpretation?

1. When the plain sense of Scripture makes common sense, we seek no other sense.
2. We accept the primary, ordinary, usual, literal meaning of the text unless the facts of the immediate context clearly indicate otherwise.
3. We resist going beyond the literal meaning of the words and context unless warranted by the text.[3]

Dr. Ron Rhodes, author and president of Reasoning from the Scriptures Ministries, expounds further on the necessity of such consistency when interpreting Scripture:

> Let's remember that the historical-grammatical method enables us to understand all the attributes of God, the absolute deity of Jesus Christ, the deity and personhood of the Holy Spirit, the doctrine of humankind's fall into sin, the gospel of salvation by grace through faith, a future judgment for humankind, and an afterlife involving heaven for the saved and hell for the unsaved. *The same historical-grammatical method reveals a distinction in Scripture between Israel and the church, and the future fulfillment of the Abrahamic and Davidic covenants in Israel in the millen-nial kingdom.* We cannot use the historical-grammatical method when convenient to our theological position and then switch to allegory when it isn't convenient. We must *consistently* use the historical-grammatical method.[4] (emphasis in original)

The gospel of salvation, as Paul describes in Ephesians 2:1–10, is far greater than anything humans could ever have devised on their own.

Apart from divine revelation, who would've ever come up with the idea of receiving forgiveness simply because of God's great mercy, grace, and love apart from any works on our part? That goes against all that we experience in life.

Likewise, as we dig deeper into the personification of Jesus in the book of Proverbs, we learn that Wisdom invites us to a lavish feast, the likes of which we can only imagine this side of glory. It's not that a book written three thousand years ago speaks directly to the imminent expectation of Jesus' appearing; it does not. However, as we dig deeper into the wisdom as revealed on its pages, we will see that our hope perfectly aligns with the words of Solomon in many ways, which is the purpose of this section.

Chapter 1

WISDOM PRIORITIZES THE WORDS OF THE BIBLICAL TEXT

Words are the units of thought in most of our thinking and writing; they are the bricks of our conceptual formulation. Any serious study of Holy Scripture must engage in the study of words.[5]

—Bernard Ramm, *Protestant Biblical Interpretation*

It's happened more times than I care to admit. I think I'm following the instructions as I assemble a piece of patio furniture or another large, do-it-yourself purchase, but I overlook a key detail or step, which causes me to have to start over—or at least redo much of my work. It always happens because I don't pay attention to *all* the words. I assume I know what I'm doing, but I later discover that I've skipped past a step that's essential to completing the project.

This lesson applies rather well to Scripture, doesn't it? If we build our beliefs upon what we *think* God's Word says, we'll certainly miss key aspects of its message. When we follow the path the words on the pages of our Bibles take us, we gain insight into our faith as well as into God's ways and character. If, in our haste, we assume what the words say (my most common mistake when I put things together), we're led astray.

The book of Proverbs, the majority of which Solomon likely wrote, is remarkably clear: *Wisdom comes to us through the words of Scripture.* They are the vehicles through which we comprehend eternal truths as well as our hope in Jesus' appearing. If we're to understand God's Word, we must pay attention to how it imparts truths to us, then follow the paths where the text takes us. *Wisdom teaches us that words matter.*

Pay Attention to the Words

The book of Proverbs repeatedly reinforces the close correlation between words and insight regarding the Lord's ways. The first chapter shouts with the message that *we must pay attention to the words of the biblical text if we're to grow in wisdom*:

> The proverbs of Solomon, son of David, king of Israel:
> To know wisdom and instruction,
> to understand **words** of insight. (1:1–2, emphasis added)

> Let the wise hear and increase in learning,
> and the one who understands obtain guidance,
> to understand a proverb and a saying,
> the **words** of the wise and their riddles. (1:5–6, emphasis added)

> If you turn at my reproof,
> behold, I will pour out my spirit to you;
> I will make my **words** known to you. (1:23, emphasis added)

Solomon continues to emphasize the necessity of discovering the ways of the Lord in chapter 2:

> My son, if you receive my words
> and treasure up my commandments with you,
> making your ear attentive to wisdom
> and inclining your heart to understanding. (2:1–2)

The connection is unmistakable; the ancient king intricately links words with our growth in understanding God and His ways. *The two are inseparable.* The historical-grammatical method of biblical interpretation, as discussed in the introduction to this section, relies entirely upon the words of the text as well as the context, which includes the surrounding verses, the book, and the entire Scripture.

The Lord is the source of all biblical wisdom, and He communicates this insight to us through what we read on the pages of Scripture. Notice the emphasis of Proverbs 2:6: "For the Lord gives wisdom; from his mouth come knowledge and understanding."

Each time I read the above verse, I'm reminded of what Paul wrote in 2 Timothy 3:16–17: "All Scripture is breathed out by God and profitable for teaching, for reproof, for correction, and for training in righteousness, that the man of God may be complete, equipped for every good work."

It's likely the apostle had Proverbs 2:6 in mind when he wrote the above verses, which have become our standard for understanding the value of God's inspired Word. We might sum it up this way:

God's wisdom comes to us today through the inspired text of Scripture, which we have in our own language on the pages of our Bibles. We can trust all the words of Scripture and rely on what its authors, under the direction of the Holy Spirit, wrote. It's truly God's wisdom for us.

The Reformers—in particular, Martin Luther—summed up this thought with two principles that highlight both the essential nature of words and their context in the whole of God's Word:

1. *Sola Scriptura*: A Latin phrase signifying that all our beliefs and practices must come from the Bible and no other source.
2. Scripture interprets Scripture: This indicates that the clearer passages of Scripture enable us to better understand those that are less clear. We must assume that Scripture never contradicts itself.

Why is it important to emphasize that wisdom comes our way through the words of Scripture? Because many saints trust what the Lord reveals regarding their salvation, but fail to value the words of Bible prophecy in a similar fashion.

When it comes to the matter of eternal life, they rely solely on the words of Scripture and nothing else. Yet when it comes to Israel and what the New Testament says about the nation's future, they accept symbolic interpretations that are based on subjective human wisdom rather than on what the Holy Spirit inspired the prophets to write. As a result, differing viewpoints of the future abound among those who take such an approach to Bible prophecy.

I once heard a sermon on Acts 1:6–11, which illustrates the failure to heed the phrasing of the scriptural text regarding future matters. When the pastor initially read the passage, he misread the disciples' question to Jesus. I initially assumed he had just inadvertently confused the words. But after it became clear that he didn't believe in Israel's future restoration as a nation; I paid closer attention to how he again changed the question from "Lord, will you at this time restore the kingdom **to** Israel?" to, "Lord, will you at this time restore the kingdom **of** Israel?" (Acts 1:6, emphasis added).

Do you see how changing one small word made the question about restoring a kingdom *similar* to what the Lord had promised His people rather than reestablishing a glorious realm specifically for Israel? A seemingly insignificant change in the wording of the text made the passage support Replacement Theology rather than the true assumption behind the disciples' inquiry.

The disciples sought clarification regarding the Lord's promise to Israel, not the establishment of something similar to it such as the Church.

Words matter! This is true about our hope of eternal life as well as the specifics of what's ahead for us.

The Pursuit of Wisdom

The wide availability of Scripture around the world exceeds anything the apostles could have imagined in the first century AD. The words of Proverbs 8:1 are coming to life in our day as never before: "Does not wisdom call? Does not understanding raise her voice?"

Why is it, then, that believers scatter in so many directions despite the clarity of God's Word? This happens in regard to the gospel and matters related to eternal security. It's also the case with Bible prophecy.

It would take an entire book, a lengthy one at that, to fully answer that question. However, I'm convinced the problem begins with a lack of devotion to what the words of Scripture reveal about God, His ways, and His wisdom. Many rely on human wisdom and thus fail to pursue the understanding that comes from studying the Bible for themselves. They base their beliefs on what their pastor says rather than on what they read in their Bibles.

As a child, I attended the AWANA ("Approved Workmen Are Not Ashamed") discipleship program for several years. I kept a plaque in my bedroom with these words from 2 Timothy 2:15, the foundation of the program: "Study to shew thyself approved unto God, a workman that needeth not to be ashamed, rightly dividing the word of truth" (KJV).

Even as an adult, this verse continues to impress upon my heart the importance of diligently pursuing the correct understanding of Scripture. While modern versions of the Bible correctly translate the last phrase of the verse as "rightly handling the word of truth," the Greek word, *ortho-tomeo*, signifies cutting in a "straight line"—or, as the King James Version translates, "rightly dividing the word of truth." The word denotes handling God's Word with accuracy.

There is a right way and a wrong way to interpret God's Word, which means we must always examine what others say, or write, in light of what we read on its pages. *What other guide do we have?*

Paul describes one who correctly interprets "the word of truth" as a "workman," or a laborer. Grasping the wisdom of God's revelation surely involves the Holy Spirit, who indwells all New Testament saints. However, we must also be devoted students of Scripture; *we must pursue its wisdom.* It requires effort on our part. Perhaps Solomon had something similar in mind when he wrote these words: "It is the glory of God to conceal things, but the glory of kings is to search things out" (Proverbs 25:2).

Yes, of course, many young children can understand the gospel—and many come to saving faith in Jesus at an early age. I first responded to its saving message at age six, but now, many decades later, my understanding of God's redeeming mercies, love, and grace continues to deepen. I continually find new insights that I previously overlooked. It's become a never-ending pursuit and expansion of biblical wisdom in regard to my redemption.

Solomon captured this truth well in Proverbs 2:3–5:

Yes, if you call out for insight
and raise your voice for understanding,
if you seek it like silver
and search for it as for hidden treasures,
then you will understand the fear of the Lord
and find the knowledge of God.

Most believers today fail to pursue wisdom. They accept what they hear or read without verifying the message against what the Bible says. As a result, false teachings abound, particularly concerning Bible prophecy.

When we chase after wisdom as revealed in God's Word, it always leads us to Jesus in ways that magnify His Name, uphold the integrity of His revelation to us, and glorify His kingdom. And, as we will see, this pursuit verifies our hope in Jesus' soon appearing.

How Do We Grow in God's Wisdom?

Every believer possesses some degree of God's wisdom, but not every saint pursues a deeper understanding of it. Sadly, many ignore Scripture while others rely solely on what others tell them it says. The failure of Christians to test everything they hear or read against the words of the Bible allows false teachings to flourish.

Proverbs 8 concludes with a blessing for all who "daily" seek the Lord and His wisdom. Life doesn't end well for those who spurn Him and His words. Those who find the Savior receive a rich reward, as described in verses 32–36:

And now, O sons, listen to me:
blessed are those who keep my ways.
Hear instruction and be wise,
and do not neglect it.
Blessed is the one who listens to me,
watching daily at my gates,

waiting beside my doors.
For whoever finds me finds life
and obtains favor from the Lord,
but he who fails to find me injures himself;
all who hate me love death.

Our quest for biblical wisdom is not at all about earning eternal life or obtaining God's favor. The Bible clearly states that forgiveness of our sins—our salvation—comes solely by grace through faith: "For by grace you have been saved through faith. And this is not your own doing; it is the gift of God, not a result of works, so that no one may boast" (Ephesians 2:8–9).

We all start out as "by nature children of wrath" until God intervenes by making "us alive together with Christ" (Ephesians 2:1–5). We don't earn our salvation in any way, shape, or form. It's all a gift of grace.

However, as New Testament saints, the promise of Proverbs 8 is that we can discover many riches when we develop a close walk with Jesus, particularly when we pay close attention to the wealth of wisdom throughout Scripture.

Equating Jesus with wisdom isn't just an Old Testament understanding that no longer applies. In Colossians 2:1–3, Paul also prays for believers to obtain a deeper understanding of God's wisdom:

For I want you to know how great a struggle I have for you and for those at Laodicea and for all who have not seen me face to face, that their hearts may be encouraged, being knit together in love, to reach all the riches of full assurance of understanding and the knowledge of God's mystery, which is Christ, in whom are hidden all the treasures of wisdom and knowledge.

Bibles with Jesus' words printed in red ink are helpful, but in reality, every word of every verse, from Genesis 1:1 to Revelation 22:21, emanates from Him. There's no substitute for studying Scripture and verifying what we read and hear from other sources (including this book) against what's on the pages of our Bibles. This is how we continue to grow in our walk with the Lord.

The wisdom that comes from above aligns with God's Word in all areas, including eschatology, the study of end-time matters. It signifies that we value the insight Jesus imparts regarding Bible prophecy rather than the beliefs of those who apply their own understanding to the texts.

How do we grow in wisdom? By immersing our hearts and minds in Scripture daily, with an attitude of submission to what the words reveal. We value Jesus' words because they're the building blocks of biblical understanding—whether understanding the gospel or our "blessed hope" (Titus 2:11–14), which Paul embedded in the saving message of the cross.

ᘓᔭ Wisdom defends Bible prophecy by:

1. **Teaching us to prioritize the words of the biblical text as our sole source of wisdom pertaining to future things.**

Chapter 2

WISDOM AFFIRMS SCRIPTURE'S INTEGRITY

When we say the Bible is without error, or completely true in all that it says, we mean there are no statements in the Bible which are falsely reported and no teachings which are inaccurate. Every statement, every event, is recorded for us truthfully. There are no deceptions or inaccuracies, whether willful or unwilful, in the pages of Scripture.[6]

—Don Stewart, "What Is the Doctrine of Biblical Inerrancy?"

Though not readily apparent, the dismissal of God's promise to restore a kingdom to Israel represents a backdoor assault on the integrity of Scripture. It begins a slow erosion that, over time, diminishes the Bible's trustworthiness in the minds of many. Replacement Theology, the claim that God has rejected Israel, over time creates an atmosphere conducive to adopting the world's standards of morality by slowly chipping away at the Church's sole dependence on the meaning of the *words* in our Bibles for all matters of faith and practice.

Our belief in God's restoration of Israel, the heart of modern-day premillennialism, finds its basis in a literal understanding of a great many biblical texts. What reason do we have to depart from the clear intent of the authors of these passages? And if we do so, what other basis do we have than subjective human reasoning?

If we abandon the meaning of the words of Scripture, aren't we just left with opinions about each passage's meaning? What's more, there's no agreement among those who subject Bible prophecy to their own understanding.

Author and theologian Erwin Lutzer's question in his book, *Forsaking Israel: How It Happened and Why It Matters*, sums up this matter the best: "If God didn't mean what He said, why didn't He say what He meant?"[7]

A famous statement defending the integrity of God's Word lends much support to Lutzer's words.

Chicago Statement on Biblical Inerrancy

In 1978, 334 Evangelicals met in Chicago and agreed to a statement affirming the inerrancy and inspiration of Scripture. This was the year I graduated from Talbot Theological Seminary and, as I recall, the integrity of the Bible was a hot-button issue at the time. My professors assigned students to read several books on the matter. In fact, I still have my copy of Harold Lindsell's *The Battle for the Bible*, which he wrote in 1976.

I am aware that a few of those who signed the Chicago statement ascribed to Replacement Theology. However, I'm also convinced that the wording of the document refutes the subjective and symbolical interpretations of biblical prophecy upon which this teaching rests.

The following is from Article VI of the statement: "We affirm that the whole of Scripture and all its parts, down to the very words of the original, were given by divine inspiration."[8]

Notice the emphasis on "words." Through the process of inspiration, the Lord worked through the human authors so they chose the wording He desired. What right do we have to change what He intended to communicate through those who penned the words of Scripture?

Article XVIII of the Chicago document further negates interpreting God's Word in ways that stray from the meaning of the biblical text:

> We affirm that the text of Scripture is to be interpreted by grammatico-historical exegesis, taking account of its literary forms and devices, and that Scripture is to interpret Scripture.[9]

Without fail, a "grammatico-historical exegesis" of texts related to Bible prophecy leads us to a premillennial understanding of Bible prophecy. It's only when we divert from this path that we see allegorical interpretations based on human wisdom rather than on the intent of the authors, which forms the errant basis for Replacement Theology.

During the years following the 1978 Chicago gathering, the vast majority of churches identifying themselves as "Evangelical" not only stood by the resulting statement of biblical inerrancy, but also affirmed adherence to a futuristic interpretation of the book of Revelation. Beliefs in the inerrancy of Scripture, premillennialism, and the pre-Tribulation Rapture remained inseparable from the proclamation of inerrancy and inspiration that came from the conference in the Windy City.

Sadly, such is no longer the case. Some places of worship today adhere to the amillennial 1833 New Hampshire Confession of Faith alongside the 1978 Chicago Statement on Biblical Inerrancy, despite the intrinsic contradiction between these two declarations of beliefs. While the latter champions historical-grammatical approach to the biblical text, the 1833 document finds its basis in Replacement Theology, which depends on retrofitting the clear meaning of prophetic texts with human wisdom.

My predisposition to defend the words of the Bible against allegorizing its prophecies intensified during the twelve months after my graduation from Talbot Seminary. During this time, I worked at the Lockman Foundation, assisting in the production of its *Exhaustive Concordance for the New American Standard Bible*. I spent days immersed in the Hebrew and Aramaic text of the Old Testament, connecting words in the original language to their English equivalents in the New American Standard Bible.

Spending forty hours a week studying the original text of the Old Testament not only greatly increased my love of the words of Scripture, but also gave me a permanent resistance to any attempt to apply symbolic meanings by allegorizing the texts. It left the following unfading impression on me:

The amazing uniformity of the Hebrew text, written over many centuries by a variety of authors and prophets, is not something I can allow theologians living thousands of years later to discredit by retrofitting its words to cancel God's solemn promises to Israel. It's clear that the Lord worked through the personalities of the writers to inspire the exact words they used to describe future events, many prophecies of which remain unfulfilled to this day.

Back then, I regarded my time at the Lockman Foundation as an unnecessary delay in reaching my goal of becoming a senior pastor. I didn't appreciate the work God was doing there to prepare me for future ministry.

"What's the big deal?" many ask. "As long as a church remains true to the gospel and its pastors carefully exegete Scripture in texts that don't pertain to future things, why should we be alarmed if they dismiss God's solemn promises to Israel?"

The Fruit of Allegorizing the Words of Scripture

Several years ago, I spent a lunchtime explaining to a local pastor the biblical necessity for the Lord to restore a future kingdom to the nation of Israel. At one point, the pastor criticized my beliefs as being out of step with popular trends in the church. He pointed to Andy Stanley, a well-known pastor in Atlanta, as an example of someone whose beliefs I should emulate. According to him, my views were out of step with more up-to-date thinking regarding the end times, including the ones this pastor from the South publicly espoused.

Stanley adheres to Replacement Theology and often asserts that Christians must "unhitch" themselves from the Old Testament. Perhaps he reasons that if the Church has inherited all of God's kingdom promises for Israel in a spiritual manner, why study its teachings and prophecies? Was this the "modern" example I was supposed to follow?

As I continue to hear reports regarding Stanley's downward slide into wokeism, his growing acceptance of those who adhere to the world's standards of morality, I think back to that past noontime conversation. Stanley's continued drift away from the truths of Scripture is evident by his response to criticism of his sermon series, "The Bible Told Me So":

I wanted educated, dechurched millennials to know that I knew that those who supposedly know everything are convinced there

26

was no worldwide flood or Hebrew migration from Egypt. While addressing them directly, I gave them the benefit of the doubt to make the following point: Even if those events never occurred, it does nothing to undermine the evidence supporting the resurrection of Jesus and thus the claims he made about himself.[10]

It's admirable that Stanley wants to reach Millennials with the saving message of the gospel, but at what price? How does one reconcile Jesus' claim to be God with His supposed mistaken beliefs regarding Creation, the Flood, and Moses, who recorded these events? To give the unsaved the "benefit of the doubt" regarding events Jesus confirmed during His ministry undermines His credibility as our Savior. How can it not?

In a video I recently watched on YouTube, Tom Hughes, former pastor and Bible prophecy expert, quoted Andy Stanley as saying, "I'm really on a crusade to help the church specifically step back away from a text-based faith."

"What text?" Hughes responded. "Is he saying we must step away from a Bible-based faith? He's already said that 'we must unhitch ourselves from the Old Testament.'"

Telling people they don't have to believe the Bible is highly problematic. Yes, God saves us completely apart from anything within ourselves (Ephesians 2:1–10). However, Paul also wrote that "faith comes from hearing, and hearing through the word of Christ" (Romans 10:17). Isn't it contradictory to tell the unsaved to base their hope on Scripture, while at the same time implying that we must ignore the Lord's promises to restore a kingdom to Israel?

The failure to uphold the integrity of God's Word, such as what's reflected in Stanley's approach, results in several undesirable consequences for those who follow this path.

1. It Leads to Greater Depths of False Teaching

Replacement Theology provides the basis for many other teachings that take believers farther away from biblical wisdom. Its most popular offspring, Dominion Theology, teaches that the church, not Jesus, will inaugurate the millennial conditions on earth. This extreme position is a logical outcome of saying the Church is now God's kingdom and Jesus is ruling His kingdom despite being absent from the earth. Further, it contradicts what Paul wrote about Jesus' preeminence in Colossians 1:15–20.

Dominion Theology also represents an open attack on the reliability of Scripture, because it accepts new revelation to the church. That clearly opposes what God has already said through His prophets.

Preterism, another child of Replacement Theology, became popular during the 1500s as the Catholic Church used it to respond to the Reformers' insistence that the pope was the Antichrist. Like its sibling, Dominion Theology, such an interpretation of prophecy contradicts the clear words of Scripture, which causes others to adhere to deviant interpretations in areas not related to future things.

Adherents of Preterism claim Jesus returned to earth in AD 70 with the fulfillment of **all** Bible prophecy reaching fulfillment during the first century AD. A milder form of it places our receipt of immortal bodies at Jesus' end-of-the-age return by combining it with the Rapture.

2. It Opens the Door to Wokeism

The problem with accepting that the words on the pages of Scripture can mean something different than what its authors originally intended is this: It opens the door for others to use that same approach in matters pertaining to the LGBQT+ agenda and the killing of children in the womb.

For example, if one can say God has rejected Israel despite Paul's clear assertion to the contrary in Romans 11:1–2, isn't it easy to assume others might apply the same principle of interpretation to what he wrote about homosexuality? Doesn't this open the door for alternate types of behavior the apostle specifically prohibits?

Andy Stanley has become Exhibit A for how Replacement Theology starts one down the path to Wokeism and the acceptance of many beliefs and behaviors that God hates. Though Stanley stops far short of endorsing the entire LGBQT+ agenda, his recent statements illuminate the path to make it easier for others to go there.

How can we not sound the alarm when Stanley, perhaps the most skilled and influential "evangelical" preacher in America, seeks to move the Church away from its firm foundation upon the Word of God?

Pastor Tom Hughes made the following comment in the video I mentioned earlier referring to Stanley's desire to move the Church away from its biblical moorings: "This is bad; this is really bad!"

I agree!

3. It Deprives Believers of the Refuge Provided by Bible Prophecy

Bible prophecy provides us with great encouragement for the perilous times in which we live. There's no greater comfort for our day than what Scripture reveals about our future.

I couldn't even begin to cope with all I see happening around us apart from what the Bible teaches about the hereafter. Jesus is my strong tower of refuge; His Word is what keeps me sane, because I know He will intervene in this world in the near future. He is coming soon to take me home, and after that, He will punish the great wickedness that's overtaking humanity.

Pastors who remain silent about Bible prophecy and the Rapture or proclaim a variant of Replacement Theology deprive those under their care of knowing about the only safe refuge available during these lawless and violent times. They lead saints away from the "strong tower" (Proverbs 18:10), that of Jesus and His Word, to sandcastles that will soon disappear amid the raging waves of the sea during the perilous times between now and Jesus' imminent appearing.

With each passing month, it becomes increasingly apparent just how much we need the hope of Jesus' any-moment return and His subsequent judgment of the great wickedness prevalent in our world. While it's true that some saints don't want to hear about our anticipation of meeting Jesus in the air, many of us treasure this expectation and we can't imagine coping with these perilous times without it.

4. It Fosters an Unbiblical Worldview

Many pastors today regard Bible prophecy as a threat to their ministry and treat the Rapture as an idea far too radical to even address from the pulpit. People, they fear, might stop attending services or giving tithes and offerings if they dare to mention our "blessed hope" (Titus 2:11–14) or the promise that the Lord will give us immortal bodies at His appearing.

The lack of guidance in connecting what the Bible says about the age in which we live leads to many false assumptions about it. This unawareness of current events, together with a lack of understanding of how the emergence of Israel as nation is necessary for the fulfillment of Bible prophecy, leads many to an unbiblical worldview. This faulty perspective is seen in the following ways within the Christian community:

- A disdain for Israel, which for many has become a breeding ground for anti-Semitism. Those who believe God rejected the nation long ago fail to recognize Israel's God-given right to the Land.
- An adherence to the normality bias that's so prevalent in our day, especially in America. This causes many saints to ignore the storm clouds of the Tribulation period that darken the horizon and make long-term plans, assuming nothing will interfere with their aspirations.
- A lack of discernment that results in Christians supporting candidates who passionately endorse anti-biblical standards of decency and behavior.

As a small boy, I jumped to my feet while singing, "I stand alone on the Word of God, the B-I-B-L-E." How does this relate to my passion for defending premillennialism against the wiles of Replacement Theology? Because the latter significantly harms the Body of Christ in at least two ways:

- It moves followers of Jesus away from depending on Scripture as the basis for all matters pertaining to faith and practice.
- It harms the saints by redirecting their hope of glory to the things of this life and by opening their minds to the wokeism that's so prevalent in the world.

❧ Wisdom defends Bible prophecy by:

1. Teaching us to prioritize the words of the biblical text as our sole source of wisdom pertaining to future things.
2. Upholding the original intent of the authors of Scripture to whom the Lord revealed His plans for the ages.

Chapter 3

WISDOM MAGNIFIES
JESUS' NAME

One of the greatest of the foundational doctrines of Christianity—
the prophecy about the literal Second Coming of Christ to establish
his kingdom—has unfortunately been neglected by many within the
body of believers in our generation. However, the prophecy about
Christ's return is presented throughout the Word of God.[11]

—Grant R. Jeffrey, *Triumphant Return*

The most grievous casualty of the current siege against Bible prophecy
has been the magnificence of Jesus' Name. It's not that any teaching
can take away from His splendor, but all teachings related to Replacement Theology or amillennialism portray Him in way that falls far short
of the glory ascribed to Him on the pages of God's Word.

As an example, those who attack the futuristic interpretation of the
book of Revelation fail to see how it exalts Him from beginning to end.
The very first words of that book provide its theme: "The revelation of
Jesus Christ" (Revelation 1:1).

The grand culmination of Revelation is Jesus' spectacularly glorious
return to the earth at the end of the Tribulation to establish His thousand-year rule over the nations (Revelation 19:11–20:4). Everything in
the book leads up to this; every verse drips with the notion of His power
and points us to His exaltation over all the kingdoms that now rebel
against Him and curse His Name.

The Apostle Paul states that our Savior's reign over all peoples on planet earth will result in His final defeat of His enemies, which will make possible the eternal state when death, sin, and pain will no longer exist.

> For he must reign until he has put all his enemies under his feet. The last enemy to be destroyed is death. For "God has put all things in subjection under his feet." But when it says, "all things are put in subjection," it is plain that he is excepted who put all things in subjection under him. When all things are subjected to him, then the Son himself will also be subjected to him who put all things in subjection under him, that God may be all in all. (1 Corinthians 15:25–28)

Throughout my years of schooling, I became quite familiar with the word "prerequisite." To be allowed to take a class I desired, I first had to enroll in one or more other courses—the prerequisites. In the above passage, Paul reveals a prerequisite for the eternal state, Jesus' millennial reign during which all things will be subject to His power. His thousand-year rule at a time when sin and death occur must happen before the glorious picture of the eternal state that John paints for us in Revelation chapters 21–22.

Those who skip from the Church Age to the white throne judgment described in Revelation 20:11–15 and the inauguration of the eternal state greatly misunderstand Scripture and, in particular, the message of the apocalypse.

Perhaps even more significant, their mistaken understanding of the Millennium often glorifies the Church much more than it does the Savior.

The Psalms repeatedly say Jesus' thousand-year rule will be a time of endless worship and singing praises to Him. The verses below reflect the worship that will resound throughout the earth during that time:

> Sing praises to God, sing praises!
> Sing praises to our King, sing praises!
> For God is the King of all the earth;

sing praises with a psalm!
God reigns over the nations;
God sits on his holy throne. (Psalm 47:5–8)

All the nations you have made shall come
and worship before you, O Lord,
and shall glorify your name. (Psalm 86:9)

We see a similar theme throughout many of the other Psalms (9:11; 24:7–10; 66:32–35; 95:1–3; 96:1–10; 98:1–10; 99:1–5). The Gospels tell of Jesus' humble birth, the life He lived in relative obscurity, His submission to death on the cross for our sake, and then of His resurrection. In all these things, He fulfilled specific prophecies from the Old Testament.

The Most Exhilarating Event in Human History

Words fail to adequately describe the splendor and dazzling majesty of His Second Advent that will begin with His glorious return to earth and continue throughout a kingdom that will exceed anything the world has ever known in grandeur, power, and righteousness.

The wisdom that resounds throughout God's Word shouts that Jesus will surely intervene in our world again, beginning with the Rapture of the Church. This firm understanding, rooted Scripture, builds through its pages to the glorious finale recorded in the closing chapters of Revelation.

The most exhilarating event in all of human history lies in the future: Jesus' Second Coming. All of God's Word builds to this moment. Pastor and author Ray C. Stedman wrote about His return to the earth, which Stedman introduced as "the most prophesied event in the Bible":

Then comes a moment that marks the end of His secret presence—the brilliant, globally visible event of His appearance when Jesus ends the secrecy of His presence and the whole world suddenly sees Him. This is the outshining of His presence before a thunderstruck world.[12]

Jesus states His return to earth will take place after a time of "great tribulation" that clearly hasn't yet happened (Matthew 24:21). The glorious picture the Lord paints of His Second Coming in Matthew 24:29–31 stretches the imagination to its breaking point. Amid earth's darkness, the world will see the brilliance of Jesus and His host riding on horseback across the sky (see also Revelation 19:11–16).

Everyone on earth will witness this overwhelming display of power, majesty, and glory that will pierce through the nations nestled in darkness. They will see Jesus in all His splendor and most will wail in grief realizing they have believed Satan's lies, but it will be too late for them (see Revelation 1:7).

Imagine watching fireworks when the sky suddenly grows dark and remains so for several minutes before the grand finale. However, this is no ordinary display; the grand finale continues nonstop for longer than ten hours. The astonishing wonder of Jesus' return to earth will far exceed such a picture.

Those who consider Jesus' return to the earth a perfunctory wrap-up of human history do a great disservice to the Savior as well as to God's Word. Can you imagine an event so amazing that the Lord was talking about it with Enoch before the Noahic Flood (Jude 14–15)? If Christ's return was so important that He would reveal its grandeur thousands of years before it was to happen, we know the pictures of it in Matthew 24:29–31 and Revelation 19:11–16 only give us a hint of the surpassing glory it will bring to the Savior.

It's my contention that today's popular portrayal of a dull end-of-the-age return of Jesus is not only unbiblical, but severely downplays the magnificence ascribed to His return in the book of Revelation as well as throughout Scripture. Such teaching not only attacks Scripture's integrity, but it also severely diminishes the all-powerful and exalted image of the Savior we see throughout its pages.

Biblical wisdom, on the other hand magnifies the Savior, and for several reasons:

1. Biblical wisdom keeps our hope of glory focused on Jesus, not on an event. Those who adhere to Replacement Theology in its many forms dishonor Jesus in no small way by pushing our hope away from His unveiling in glory to an event that's remarkably sterile compared with how Scripture describes His return to earth. Their view of the Second Coming becomes a perfunctory wrap-up of history just before the eternal state rather than the spectacular event revealed throughout God's Word.

The amillennial 1833 New Hampshire Confession of Faith perfectly sums up this bland—and, might I add, totally unbiblical—view of the Second Coming. Yes, it includes Jesus' return to the earth, but it becomes anticlimactic against the backdrop of a far-distant occurrence, during which time God simultaneously raises saints and sinners, separates them, and judges them accordingly. Our hope dwindles to an ordinary event rather than Jesus' breathtakingly glorious ride through the sky, His defeat of all the armies arrayed against Him, and the establishment of His rule upon the earth.

Can you see how a dull, errant wrap-up of human history degrades the exaltation we see in the Bible's picture of Jesus at His Second Coming? He is "the author and finisher of our faith" (Hebrews 12:2, KJV). He will complete our redemption when He gives us immortal and imperishable bodies at His appearing (1 Corinthians 15:47–55).

We must not separate the gospel from our anticipation of meeting Jesus in the air (1 Thessalonians 4:17). In 1 Corinthians 15:1–19, the Apostle Paul connects our future resurrection with that of Jesus, with the implication that they're both essential for our understanding of the gospel.

Yes, the Rapture is an event, but it also encapsulates our joyous expectation of meeting Jesus in the air, fixes our hope solely upon Him, and exalts Him. Our focus thus becomes that of eagerly awaiting "a Savior, the Lord Jesus Christ, who will transform our lowly body to by like his glorious body" (Philippians 3:20–21).

Biblically sound wisdom makes Jesus and His appearing the focus of our expectation of glory, not a far-distant event that has no relevance to our daily lives.

2. **Biblical wisdom magnifies Jesus, not the Church.** In several conversations with those who adhere to Replacement Theology or its offshoot, Preterism, I've often heard words exalting the Church above Jesus'

Name. At first, I wouldn't attribute any particular significance to these statements, but over time I came to regard the words as symptomatic of an undue exaltation of the Church and a lessening of Jesus' vital role in our future. I see a direct correlation between that and what they believe about future things.

Those who say the Church is now God's kingdom in fulfillment of prophetic passages such as Psalm 2 or Revelation 20:1–10 diminish the biblical picture of Jesus as the culmination of human history. They shift the focus to the Church and thus away from Him.

As we will expand upon in chapter 13, the Bible says when Jesus rules over planet earth, wars, ethnic strife, wickedness, extreme injustice, deception, lawlessness, and widespread government corruption will not exist. The prevalence of these things in our day tells us that Jesus' reign over the nations, including a restored Israel, surely awaits a future day. Isn't it demeaning to Jesus to say He now fulfills the words of Psalm 2 when these conditions and events characterize our world? Yes, absolutely. The perilous times of our day shout the message that Jesus' kingdom awaits fulfillment.

Only Jesus can initiate this still-future time of righteousness and peace on the earth. This isn't our current experience, nor is it something a woefully divided and worldly Church can accomplish in the future.

The wisdom that comes from above speaks to the acclaim that Jesus will receive when the Church roars with thunderous praise for Him in Heaven and then returns with Him to set up a kingdom, during which time the nations of the world will worship Him for a thousand years (see Revelation 19:1–8). This jubilant celebration of Jesus' greatness lies in our future.

The words of Daniel 7:27 aptly sum up what Jesus' thousand-year rule will mean for us and the praise that will resound through the earth:

And the kingdom and the dominion
and the greatness of the kingdoms under the whole heaven
shall be given to the people of the saints of the Most High;
his kingdom shall be an everlasting kingdom,
and all dominions shall serve and obey him.

Please don't let anyone tell you this has already happened. It most certainly awaits a future fulfillment when "all dominions shall serve and obey him." The above verse doesn't refer to the Church Age, but represents the earth after the Lord returns to rule over the nations.

༼✑ *Wisdom defends Bible prophecy by:*

1. Teaching us to prioritize the words of the biblical text as our sole source of wisdom pertaining to future things.
2. Upholding the original intent of the authors of Scripture to whom the Lord revealed His plans for the ages.
3. Magnifying Jesus as the One who will defeat death and make possible the eternal state.

Chapter 4

WISDOM SUBSTANTIATES OUR HOPE

In the Bible, the word translated "fear" can mean several things. It can refer to the terror one feels in a frightening situation (Deuteronomy 2:25). It can mean "respect" in the way a servant fears his master and serves him faithfully (Joshua 24:14). Fear can also denote the reverence or awe a person feels in the presence of greatness (Isaiah 6:5). The fear of the Lord is a combination of all of these.[13]

—www.gotquestions.org

I t's one of the more profound statements in the book of Proverbs, but perhaps the most misunderstood: "The fear of the Lord is the beginning of knowledge" (1:7). But how is that possible? Solomon repeats this message in Proverbs 9:10, and we find further insight from the ancient king in the words of Proverbs 15:33: "The fear of the Lord is instruction in wisdom, and humility comes before honor."

Is this just an Old Testament concept with no relevance for New Testament saints?

No, it's not. In fact, Paul included it in his instructions regarding household relationships: "Bondservants, obey in everything those who are your earthly masters, not by way of eye-service, as people-pleasers, but with sincerity of heart, fearing the Lord" (Colossians 3:22).

While Paul's words apply directly to believing slaves of his day, all of his instructions in this verse apply for our day as well. And didn't Jesus say, "Do not fear those who kill the body but cannot kill the soul. Rather

fear him who can destroy both soul and body in hell" (Matthew 10:28, emphasis added)?

Furthermore, a proper understanding of the "fear of the Lord" reveals that it has much relevance to New Testament saints.

In Revelation 19:4–6, a voice from the throne room of the Father equates the throng of believers jubilantly praising Him with those "who fear him." Although the majority of references to it come from the Psalms and Proverbs, we shouldn't dismiss the "fear of the Lord" as something strictly Old Testament that doesn't apply today. Someday, as we worship the Lord with immortal and glorified bodies, we will hear an approving voice encouraging us to continue praising the Father as those "who fear him."

All believers possess some degree of the fear of the Lord. With the arrival of saving faith, we recognize our need of forgiveness for our sins to avoid God's future judgment of them. Realizing what will happen if we reject Jesus' gracious offer of forgiveness also works for our benefit because it causes us to place all our hope in Him.

Until the past couple of years, I didn't fully understand what it meant to fear the Lord. I realized those who reject the Savior have much reason to be afraid because of God's judgment of their sins, but I didn't know what it meant for me as a justified saint with no prospect whatsoever of condemnation in my future (Romans 8:1).

However, as my understanding of Scripture has deepened in recent years, so has my grasp of what it means to fear the Lord. I've discovered there's an advantage that flows to us as the redeemed from a deeper understanding of what it means. How does this relate to Bible prophecy? I believe such reverence for Him substantiates our hope for the following reasons.

Fear of the Lord Leads to the Source of Wisdom

Because I enjoy communicating with words, most folks might not expect that I also love working with numbers. After receiving an MBA with an emphasis in finance and accounting, I enjoyed a lengthy career as a financial analyst in the business world before I went into writing. Number-crunching proved to be an excellent fit.

Don't panic; I'm not about to take you deep into the realm of mathematics. However, just as equations are important for budgets and financial forecasts, they also help us better understand what it means to fear the Lord. The books of Psalms and Proverbs provide many statements in which the word "is" expands our grasp of what fearing the Lord signifies for our daily lives.

Let's begin with Psalm 111:10: "The fear of the Lord is the beginning of wisdom; all those who practice it have a good understanding. His praise endures forever!"

The fear of the Lord opens the door to wisdom, which leads to greater insight into God's revelation recorded on the pages of Scripture. Isn't it amazing that David points to those "who practice it [fearing the Lord]" as having "a good understanding?" It's something that not only places us on the path of wisdom, but increases our insight into the things of God.

In Psalm 112:1, the psalmist expresses God's blessing for those who demonstrate the fear of the Lord: "Praise the Lord! Blessed is the man who fears the Lord, who greatly **delights** in his commandments!" (emphasis added).

The remainder of Psalm 112 elaborates on the blessings that flow to those with the qualities put forward in the first verse.

A proper understanding of what it means to fear the Lord causes us to cherish the words of Scripture, leading us to its source, the Lord Jesus. He is the personification of Wisdom, through whom God has spoken to us directly (Hebrews 1:1–2).

A lack of this attribute—that is, not having a fear of the Lord—has the opposite effect on a believer's life. In Proverbs 28:14, we see the opposite of fearing the Lord is a hardening of the heart: "Blessed is the one who fears the Lord always, but whoever hardens his heart will fall into calamity."

So not only does fearing the Lord place us on the path of wisdom in respect to God's Word, but it also keeps our hearts open to its teachings.

Fear of the Lord Nurtures Hatred of Evil

The fear of the Lord produces a hatred for the vileness, lawlessness, violence, and rampant deception that's so prevalent in our world. It doesn't imply that we are sinless—of course we aren't. It rather pertains to our *attitude* about that evil. We see this theme throughout the book of Proverbs, such as in 8:13: "The fear of the Lord is hatred of evil. Pride and arrogance and the way of evil and perverted speech I hate."

In Psalm 36:1–3, David describes the downward progression of someone who lacks a proper fear of the Lord: "Transgression speaks to the wicked deep in his heart; there is no fear of God before his eyes. For he flatters himself in his own eyes that his iniquity cannot be found out and hated. The words of his mouth are trouble and deceit; he has ceased to act wisely and do good."

If the wicked have no fear of the Lord, doesn't that imply it's a quality those who love Him possess? In Romans 3:18, Paul quoted from another Psalm that describes humanity as having "no fear of God before their eyes."

If you feel repulsed by the government corruption and the killing of the innocent—two activities that characterize our day—it's a signal that you fear the Lord. The wisdom that flows from God's Word causes us to be repulsed by for the actions of those who promote the evils of our day.

I'm writing this chapter during the month of June, when parades in support of the LGBTQ+ agenda are a common sight across the world. Some of the signs associated with these lewd demonstrations openly defy the Savior. Obscene displays of support for a wholly unbiblical lifestyle often include banners declaring a love for Satan and others mocking our Savior.

The growing support of this lifestyle, along with widespread government backing for it, grieves us. I turn once again to Psalm 37:1–20, which assures us God will surely judge those who promote such wickedness. Because of that, we resist the temptation to fret and become angry as we watch evil prevail, but rest in His promise to bring justice to the earth.

Those who understand the fear of the Lord know He will judge the wicked both on earth and in eternity. They know He will pour out His wrath on the earth during the Tribulation period. Such insight results in an understanding of why He must deal with wickedness and lawlessness in the way that John witnessed and recorded in Revelation chapters 6–18.

For now, we wait for His intervention in our world, which will begin with the Rapture.

A word of caution: This doesn't give us license to lash out in anger at fellow saints who, like us, stand "holy and without blame" before the Lord (Ephesians 1:4). Many passages address forgiveness and love within the Body of Christ and, they emphasize the need for self-examination and awareness of our own sins before we confront a wayward believer.

Fear of the Lord Expands Knowledge of the Holy One

Hebrew poetry typically consists of two separate lines or sentences in which the second supports the first by:

- Repeating the same principle with different words.
- Contributing additional information.
- Expressing the opposite meaning.
- Completing the thought.[14]

This helps us understand Solomon's intent in Proverbs 9:10: "The fear of the Lord is the beginning of wisdom, and the knowledge of the Holy One is insight."

The parallelism of Hebrew poetry equates the "fear of the Lord" with the "knowledge of the Holy One." Wisdom that exhibits a proper reverence for the Lord leads to greater insight into His character. How does this relate to Bible prophecy? What we believe about the future of Israel, the Millennium, and the Rapture not only must align with the words of Scripture and exalt the Savior, but must also correspond with God's holy character. What we believe about future events must fit what the Bible reveals about Him.

Does belief in the future restoration of a kingdom to Israel fit God's attributes as revealed throughout Scripture? Yes, it does. One of the goals of the second section of this book will be to demonstrate how a proper understanding of His nature verifies our belief in it. The future of the Jewish people doesn't depend upon their behavior, but rather on

God's passion to vindicate the "holiness" of His "great name" (Ezekiel 36:23).

Picture a three-legged stool with the seat representing premillennialism and these three phrases on it legs:

- Words of Scripture
- Jesus' preeminence
- God's Holy Name

These three factors, lacking in other beliefs regarding future things, substantiate our belief that God has a prominent place for Israel in His future thousand-year rule over the nations. In chapter 10, I will show the close connection between God's holiness and the fulfillment of all His promises to the Jewish people.

In Proverbs 1:29–30, Solomon equates the lack of fear for the Lord with spurning both "knowledge" of Him and His counsel. Those with no understanding of what Scripture reveals about God are the ones most likely to depart from His ways. "Because they hated knowledge and did not choose the fear of the Lord, would have none of my counsel and despised all my reproof."

We find a similar connection between fearing the Lord and heeding His instruction in Psalm 25:12–13: "Who is the man who fears the Lord? Him will he instruct in the way that he should choose. His soul shall abide in well-being, and his offspring shall inherit the land."

Because those who fear the Lord seek His wisdom, they receive guidance, as well as more insight into His ways and purposes for us (see also Proverbs 14:2). This also substantiates our hope in what the Bible reveals about our future.

A proper fear of the Lord generates submission to what Scripture teaches, which in turn leads to deeper understanding. As discussed in chapter 2, reliance upon the intention of its authors preserves its integrity. Such respect begins with a deep reverence for its ultimate source and leads us to treat its words with respect.

Fear of the Lord Brings Blessing and Rewards

So far, we've seen that the fear of the Lord involves much more than being afraid. It also consists of being aware of His ways and nature, and of gathering understanding about Him through the words of Scripture.

But even more than that, it's also a pathway to blessings and rewards:

Blessed is the man who fears the Lord,
who greatly delights in his commandments! (Psalm 112:1)

Blessed is the one who fears the Lord always,
but whoever hardens his heart will fall into calamity. (Proverbs 28:14)

Blessed is everyone who fears the Lord,
who walks in his ways. (Proverbs 128:1)

The psalmist equates fearing the Lord with taking refuge in Him in Psalm 31:19:

Oh, how abundant is your goodness,
which you have stored up for those who fear you
and worked for those who take refuge in you,
in the sight of the children of mankind!

A continuing theme, particularly in Psalms 33–34, is God's nearness to those who fear Him.

Behold, the eye of the Lord is on those who fear him,
on those who hope in his steadfast love,
that he may deliver their soul from death
and keep them alive in famine. (Psalm 33:18–19)

The Psalms and Proverbs promise many blessings to those who fear the Lord. Such outcomes of our faith look far different now, during the

Church Age. Nonetheless, they tell us He is always near those who seek Him and the wisdom that flows from His Word. They also teach us that our experience in eternity will include many physical benefits. These will begin the moment Jesus appears to take us to the wondrous place He's now preparing for us.

Those with reverence for the Lord watch for the day when His many promises will become our experience. We anticipate His appearing because it's not only the time we see will see Him face to face, but because we'll do so in immortal bodies like His.

Fear of the Lord Points to Jesus' Example

The references to Jesus' ruling "in the fear of the Lord" bewilder me. At a minimum, they blow away our standard understanding of what it means. If Jesus Himself models this quality, how can we possibly dismiss it as irrelevant or even negative?

The writer of Hebrews penned these intriguing words about our Great High Priest: "In the days of his flesh, Jesus offered up prayers and supplications, with loud cries and tears, to him who was able to save him from death, and he was heard because of his reverence" (5:7).

Many commentators believe this refers to Jesus' prayer in Gethsemane just prior to His arrest. Author and Bible commentator Homer A. Kent Jr. offers these insightful words regarding Christ's words the night before His crucifixion:

> Christ's prayer in Gethsemane was heard (*eisakoustheis*, "harkened to") because of His godly fear. This is apparently a reference to Christ's perfect submission to God's will as He prayed, "Thy will be done." This display of absolute reverence for the Father resulted in the granting of the request.... As a perfect man His prayer was in full harmony with God's will and thus was certain of being answered.[15]

Jesus modeled the fear of the Lord through His perfect submission to the will of His Father. What's even more remarkable is that when Jesus rules over all the nations of the earth during the Millennium, He will also reign in the "fear of the Lord." Until recently, I glossed over some of the words in Isaiah 11:2–4 pertaining to Jesus' millennial rule. I have highlighted them below:

And the Spirit of the Lord shall rest upon him,
the Spirit of wisdom and understanding,
the Spirit of counsel and might,
the Spirit of knowledge and **the fear of the Lord.**
And his delight shall be in **the fear of the Lord.**
He shall not judge by what his eyes see,
or decide disputes by what his ears hear.
but with righteousness he shall judge the poor,
and decide with equity for the meek of the earth;
and he shall strike the earth with the rod of his mouth,
and with the breath of his lips he shall kill the wicked.
(emphasis added)

How did I miss these words in the past? If this is a quality Jesus will display when He rules over the nation of the earth, it negates most, if not all, of my previous thoughts about it. Certainly, the word "fear" can signify being frightened of someone or something, but that can't possibly be the case of the coming King who will destroy the kingdom of Antichrist and establish His righteous rule over the entire planet (Revelation 19:11–20:10).

Fear of the Lord Expands Understanding of Humility

This is another key to understanding what Scripture means when it exhorts us to fear the Lord. It begins with bowing to God's purposes for us—a posture Christ modeled so perfectly:

And being found in human form, he humbled himself by becoming obedient to the point of death, even death on a cross.

Therefore God has highly exalted him and bestowed on him the name that is above every name, so that at the name of Jesus every knee should bow, in heaven and on earth and under the earth, and every tongue confess that Jesus Christ is Lord, to the glory of God the Father. (Philippians 2:8–11)

Jesus Himself described the purpose of His first appearance on earth: "For even the Son of Man came not to be served but to serve, and to give his life as a ransom for many" (Mark 10:45).

Psalm 47, however, reveals the glorious outcome of Jesus' submission to His Father's will:

Clap your hands, all peoples!
Shout to God with loud songs of joy!
For the Lord, the Most High, is to be feared,
a great king over all the earth.
He subdued peoples under us,
and nations under our feet.
He chose our heritage for us,
the pride of Jacob whom he loves. Selah
God has gone up with a shout,
the Lord with the sound of a trumpet.
Sing praises to God, sing praises!
Sing praises to our King, sing praises!
For God is the King of all the earth;
sing praises with a psalm (Psalm 47:1–7)

Because Jesus humbled Himself to the will of His Father, someday everyone on earth will worship and sing praises to Him. When He is "the King of all the earth, "all dominions shall serve and obey him" (Daniel 7:27). In response to His supreme act of humility in subjecting Himself to the pain of the cross, God the Father will exalt His Son high above all the nations of this world.

For us, the fear of the Lord implies that we humble ourselves before

Him and among fellow believers in His Church. God later does any exalting that may follow: "Humble yourselves, therefore, under the mighty hand of God so that at the proper time he may exalt you, casting all your anxieties on him, because he cares for you" (1 Peter 5:6–7).

At least two things in these verses can comfort us as we wait for the Lord's appearing:

- God's hand is "mighty;" we can trust Him regardless of our circumstances.
- We can cast all our troubles upon Him because of His great love for us.

For far too long, I regarded the matter of fearing the Lord as something I would rather not try to understand. As my insight into the matter continues to grow, I see it as something that not only comforts me, but also substantiates my hope of meeting Jesus in the air in the extremely near future.

Wisdom defends Bible prophecy by:

1. Teaching us to prioritize the words of the biblical text as our sole source of wisdom pertaining to future things.
2. Upholding the original intent of the authors of Scripture to whom the Lord revealed His plans for the ages.
3. Magnifying Jesus' as the One whose future rule will make possible the defeat of death and the eternal state.
4. Establishing a proper reverence for the words of Scripture, which leads to deeper understanding of them.

Chapter 5

WISDOM CALMS
OUR ANXIETIES

I am deeply persuaded that the only solution to fear is fear. In other words, fear is defeated only by a bigger, greater fear. Here's what I mean. When the fear of God overwhelms and controls your heart, it protects you from the paralyzing and debilitating fear of other things. It's only when God looms hugely larger than anything you could ever face in this fallen world that your heart is able to experience peace even when you don't understand what is happening (and you don't have the power to solve it if you did).[16]

—Paul David Tripp, *New Morning Mercies*

There's an incredible practical side to properly understanding the fear of the Lord: *It calms our daily anxieties.* We see the connection between these seemingly divergent paths in Psalm 34:4–7:

I sought the Lord, and he answered me
and delivered me from all my fears.
Those who look to him are radiant,
and their faces shall never be ashamed.
This poor man cried, and the Lord heard him
and saved him out of all his troubles.
The angel of the Lord encamps
around those who fear him, and delivers them.

What role might the fear of the Lord have in our ongoing walk with the Lord? Author, seminary professor, and counselor Dr. Dan B. Allender provides insight into how this works for our good:

> What does it mean to fear God? It means to be anxious and eager to greet Him. It means to build our lives around the call of being His bride, to anticipate the pleasure of love and the aroma of passions. To fear God is to be consumed with His presence.
>
> If we fear God, how can we fear the vain effort of human beings and worldly institutions? After all, big fears make little fears go away. Our life might be filled with fears about a multitude of daily circumstances, but if a doctor suddenly announced that we had only six months to live due to inoperable cancer, all those daily fears would melt away before the news.[17]

As someone who has struggled with post-traumatic stress disorder (PTSD) in the past, I'm well aware that relief from deeply embedded fears doesn't happen quickly or simply by following several easy steps. In my book, *The Triumph of the Redeemed*, I devote a couple of chapters to the cause of my PTSD and how the Lord, over the course of many years, delivered me from that suffering.

However, when it comes to the daily anxieties that besiege all of us to some degree, a proper understanding of fearing the Lord alleviates them. What follows is not a step-by-step prescription, but an explanation of why such an attitude calms troubled hearts.

Fear of the Lord Teaches Us to Run to Jesus

The fear of the Lord teaches us to run to our Savior when troubles or circumstances threaten to plunge us into despair. In such instances, our natural tendency is to run away from Him, but that only intensifies our anxieties. Dr. Dan Allender helps us understand the importance of seeking the Lord the moment we begin to feel fear well up inside:

Where do we cross the line from a legitimate fear of a dangerous world to a fear that not only imprisons us but also offends God?

It has to do with *what or whom we fear*. And where does that fear drive us? Does it drive us to protect ourselves, or does it drive us to God, our Protector?...

Oddly, it is the fear of the world that drives us away from God. Fear of God strips away all other fears and compels us to deal with God, transcendent and infinitely higher than any mere mortal fear. Fear of God roots us not in our problems, but in the essence of existence.[18] (emphasis in original)

The fear of the Lord teaches us both to run and to fight. We begin by running to our Savior and the safety of His strong tower (Proverbs 18:10). There we find the courage to face our troubles and battle the devil, the one who is most often tempting us to cower in fright rather than face the dilemmas threatening to ruin our day or destroy our future.

When we're gripped with fear, our first impulse is to run away from God rather than toward Him. A proper understanding of the fear of the Lord, however, reverses this course. Why do we find relief in running to Him when we're besieged with fears? It has to do with resting in the knowledge that He cares deeply for us and has our best interests at heart.

Fear of the Lord:
A Reminder of His Great Love for Us

In Psalm 147:11, the psalmist tells us, "The Lord takes pleasure in those who fear him, in those who hope in his steadfast love." In this verse, resting in the Lord's "steadfast love" equates with fearing Him.

In the past, I've often made the dark times of my life much, much worse by doubting God's love for me. As a result, I've attempted to shoulder the entire load instead of following the advice found in 1 Peter 5:7, that of "casting all your anxieties on him, because he cares for you." I remind myself of this verse several times a week!

The reality is that the Lord loves us more than we can even imagine, and He is, at this moment, preparing a place for us in Heaven that will exceed even our most fanciful dreams. And, wonder of wonders, we are eternally secure. Nothing we do can deter the Lord from blessing us forever.

The wisdom that springs from a healthy fear of God brings us back to His eternal and unfailing love when our troubles seem far too much to bear—something that happens to all of us. Our anxieties push our thoughts away from the glorious reality that comes from seeing God for who He is and living in expectation of His imminent appearing.

> Fear distorts our perception of ourselves so that we seem weaker than we really are. It distorts the size of our problems so that they seem huge and undefeatable. But perhaps most significantly, *fear distorts our picture of God.* God seems weak, uninvolved, or uncaring in the midst of our troubles. *After all, if He were strong and concerned, He would not leave us in this mess.*
>
> Fear reverses reality by making evil seem all-conquering, and God impotent. But God is not impotent.[19]

Doesn't it seem that our problems often appear far greater than they really are, and our assessment of His strength falls far short of reality? The fear of the Lord comes to our rescue because it restores a true perspective of life based on the Lord's great love for us.

Do you see how this runs contrary to our normal way of thinking? Our first instinct when troubles generate pangs of fear is to think God no longer cares for us. However, when we run to Him and His Word, we find the needed refuge in knowing that not only does He love us, but He has the power to rescue us from perils.

Fear of the Lord Acknowledges God's Sovereignty

If anything exposes the existence of a lingering selfish agenda, it's how we respond to a perceived threat or the many injustices around us. When anger or fear, both sides of the same coin, begins to make its presence known, it stems from a desire for things to go our way rather than submit to what the Lord might have for us.

A good go-to passage when such feelings threaten to gain a foothold is 1 Peter 5:6–8:

> Humble yourselves, therefore, under the mighty hand of God so that at the proper time he may exalt you, casting all your anxieties on him, because he cares for you. Be sober-minded; be watchful. Your adversary the devil prowls around like a roaring lion, seeking someone to devour.

The phrase that often provides a sense of comfort is "the mighty hand of God." We're not just submitting our desires and aspirations to a weak sovereign who doesn't deeply care about us and our needs, but we're handing them over to the most powerful being in the universe, the One with the "mighty hand."

More than that, we can trust the Lord with all our troubles because He loves us more than we can imagine. Just think: The mighty Creator of the universe cares about each of us; it doesn't get any better than that!

Again, Dr. Dan Allender provides helpful insight:

> Fear is flight away from harm. It is the product of helplessness, weakness brought about by a feeling of inadequacy and lack of control. If we demand control and success, we will be destroyed, because in a sinful world our weaknesses will continually be exposed. But if we submit to God instead of demanding control, and serve God instead of insisting on success, then we will be changed, and our fears will dissipate. God's sovereignty is the ultimate issue as we face this choice. If we clutch desperately for success and control, we deny His power. If we exercise the privilege of submission and service, we acknowledge it.[20]

When a desire for recognition and success take center stage in our hearts, it's almost always accompanied by a desire to control things over which we have no jurisdiction. Anxiety always results from such a temporal perspective of life, because we can't influence many of the factors that affect our immediate future.

When the Lord reminds me that it's His appraisal of my ministry that matters more than anything else, I find the peace that has temporarily alluded me. How can we compare the value of His approval at the judgment seat of Christ versus anything we might receive in this life? If in the future He says, "Well done" to us, do the opinions of others really matter? This is the calm that the fear of the Lord brings to our hearts.

Fear of the Lord It Shifts Our Attention to Eternity

Correctly understood, the fear of the Lord soothes our hearts in the midst of perilous times because it directs our gaze toward eternity. It teaches us to fix our dearest aspirations on eternal matters rather than the fleeting realities of this world.

Of course, it's wise to set goals and make plans, but we must do so with an eternal perspective. God's wisdom teaches us to value eternal realities above temporal things (2 Corinthians 4:17–18). Bible prophecy assures us that those behind the violence, wickedness, corruption, and lawlessness of our day will pay a great price for their actions. The words of Ecclesiastes 8:11–13 sum up this needed dual perspective on what see today:

> Because the sentence against an evil deed is not executed speedily, the heart of the children of man is fully set to do evil. Though a sinner does evil a hundred times and prolongs his life, yet I know that it will be well with those who fear God, because they fear before him. But it will not be well with the wicked, neither will he prolong his days like a shadow, because he does not fear before God.

God's wisdom, birthed in the fear of the Lord, keeps our eyes on Him, about whom the Apostle John wrote the following: "For the testimony of Jesus is the spirit of prophecy" (Revelation 19:10).

I'm sure the many threats of pending disasters and wars I hear about daily would drive me to despair apart from what I know about God's plans for me, His Church, and the world. Those who now plot to drastically reduce the world's population and enslave those who remain alive will enjoy a degree of success during the Tribulation and possibly for a short while before it starts. But the Bible states that God will have the final say; He will destroy Satan's realm and establish His righteous rule of peace upon the earth.

We are able to sleep peacefully at night because Scripture assures us that God remains in charge despite what we see. We have no need to fret about evil people carrying out their murderous schemes because we know God is sovereign and will deal with them justly.

Imagine all the armies of the world gathered against Jerusalem with an overwhelming display of military might. Now, picture Jesus quickly wiping them out at His return to the earth—to such an extent that not one survives…not one, solitary soldier. This is the description of His Second Coming we read about in Zechariah 14:1–9 and Revelation 19:11–21. This is the power of our coming King!

The fear of the Lord calms our anxieties because it replaces them with Jesus as the object of our expectations about the future. The words of Psalm 147:11 reinforce this truth: "The Lord delights in those who fear him, who put their hope in his unfailing love."

The more we understand His "unfailing love," the greater our tendency to run to Him when troubles assail us. The Apostle Peter summed it up this way: "Humble yourselves, therefore, under the mighty hand of God so that at the proper time he may exalt you, casting all your anxieties on him, because he cares for you" (1 Peter 5:6–7).

Our humility before the Lord, a characteristic of what it means to fear Him, allows us to see that the One directing the affairs of our lives is sovereign and "mighty." It's not that we won't see the end of all our troubles, but we know a glorious future awaits with wonders we can only faintly imagine. When difficulties arise, and they will, we place our lives in the hands of the One who supremely cares for us and who will one day bring us safely home.

As strange as it may seem, fear calms the everyday anxieties we experience.

✒ *Wisdom defends Bible prophecy by:*

1. Teaching us to prioritize the words of the biblical text as our sole source of Wisdom pertaining to future things.

2. Upholding the original intent of the authors of Scripture to whom the Lord revealed His plans for the ages.

3. Magnifying Jesus' Name as the One whose future rule will make possible the defeat of death and the eternal state.

4. Establishing a proper reverence for the words of Scripture, which leads to a deeper understanding of them.

5. Teaching us to fully trust the glorious outcome of our faith when the troubles of this life expose our misplaced trust in outcomes that are often beyond our control.

Chapter 6

WISDOM EXTENDS AN EXTRAORDINARY INVITATION

If we believe, even subconsciously, that bodies and the earth and material things are unspiritual, even evil, then we will inevitably reject or spiritualize any biblical revelation about our bodily resurrection or the physical characteristics of the New Earth. That's exactly what has happened in most Christian churches, and it's a large reason for our failures to come to terms with a biblical doctrine of Heaven.[21]

—Randy Alcorn, *Heaven*

Proverbs 9 sheds valuable light on the contrast between Wisdom and the "woman Folly" identified later in the chapter. As noted in chapter 1, Jesus is the personification of Wisdom. His words are the substance of everything we can know about eternal matters.

In Proverbs 9, Solomon pictures the "woman Folly" as a prostitute whom he personifies in verses 13–18. Her loud call is much more than just an invitation to physical intimacy outside of marriage; it typifies all the many foolish paths people might travel down in this life. Peter A. Steveson, in his commentary on Proverbs, put it this way:

As the passage develops, she [the woman Folly] is seen to be an adulteress. This is an appropriate figure with which to personify folly since adultery fittingly represents the fullest degree of folly.[22]

While unfaithfulness to one's spouse is a prime example of foolishness, here, it denotes just one example of all the ways people reject the call of Wisdom.

This is also evident in the way Proverbs 7 and 8 contrasts the differences between Wisdom and Folly. Notice that after the prostitute makes her successful plea with "seductive speech" and "smooth talk" (7:21), the call of Wisdom immediately follows (8:1). (The chapter breaks noted in our versions of Scripture today weren't there when this was originally written, so this verse came immediately after the warnings concerning the wayward woman and the lure of her beauty and enticing words.)

In Proverbs 9, both Wisdom and Folly make their appeal to the "simple," those who are morally naïve and thus open to persuasion (Proverbs 9:6, 16). Because the "simple" haven't yet become fully acquainted with the understanding that flows from the words in Scripture, they remain vulnerable to making the wrong choices. As such, they need Wisdom's guidance to avoid the downward path offered by the "woman Folly."

A Lavish Feast

The lavishness of Wisdom's invitation leaps from the word picture of Proverbs 9. Her home has "seven pillars" (v. 1), which suggests a beautiful and spacious mansion. There's room for all who enter and enjoy what she has prepared.

The personification of Wisdom as a "she" is surprising at first since, in the context of Proverbs 8 and 9, it refers to Jesus. The confusion comes from the differences between the Hebrew and English languages. The following quote from the Got Questions website explains why Solomon's use of the feminine pronoun for Wisdom doesn't imply it's an actual woman preparing the banquet noted in Proverbs 9:2, but rather an "intangible quality":

In English, the word wisdom is grammatically neuter, but not so in Hebrew. The Hebrew word is *chokmoth*, and it is grammatically feminine. In Hebrew, it would have been natural to speak of wisdom as a "she."

As previously mentioned, Solomon used the literary tool of personification to extol the inanimate and abstract idea of wisdom as if it were a real person. By doing so, Solomon communicated a vivid illustration of the blessings of being wise. In personifying wisdom, it was necessary to use the appropriate pronouns. Since a person is not referred to as an "it," Wisdom as an antecedent requires feminine personal pronouns. The grammatical construction is an artifact of the process of personification. In other words, since the word wisdom is feminine (in Hebrew grammar), Wisdom personified becomes a "she" to satisfy the demands of diction—not to add information to its object.[23]

The event Wisdom is hosting consists of an extravagant feast that includes meat, wine, and bread (vv. 2–5). She has set her table with fine foods, and it's clear she has spared no expense or effort in preparing a bountiful meal for those who accept her invitation.

Wisdom sends "her young women" to the public places in the city to announce her call to enjoy what she has prepared for them. Wisdom pursues the simple so they may know the extravagance of what awaits.

This most definitely is NOT the health-and-wealth message peddled by many preachers today. The temporal blessings they offer more closely resemble those of the woman Folly in that they keep the hopes of "simple" folks tethered to earthly outcomes rather than to the riches Wisdom presents.

The contrast between Wisdom and Folly couldn't be greater. Rather than Wisdom's festal setting with joyous conversation among many fellow saints, Folly offers "stolen water" and "bread eaten in secret" (v. 17). Even though Folly's feast doesn't come close to matching the abundance of Wisdom's, Folly deceives the folks into believing what she offers is somehow "pleasant" because of its secretive nature.

Our full experience of all Jesus bestows won't happen until He calls us home either through death or when we meet Him in the air. He's preparing a place for us in His Father's house, our destination when He appears (John 14:2–3). That's when we, along with all other New Testament saints, will feast with our Savior. Doesn't this resemble the call of Wisdom in Proverbs 9:1–6?

When Christ appears, He will give us immortal and imperishable bodies just like His (1 Corinthians 15:47–55; Philippians 3:20–21). This speaks to our future glory, which Paul, despite his great suffering, put this way: "For I consider that the sufferings of this present time are not worth comparing with the glory that is to be revealed to us" (Romans 8:18).

In the meantime, the paths of those who worship and serve Jesus vary greatly. As an example, notice the wide range of experiences among the Old Testament heroes of faith listed in Hebrews 11:32–38:

> And what more shall I say? For time would fail me to tell of Gideon, Barak, Samson, Jephthah, of David and Samuel and the prophets—who through faith conquered kingdoms, enforced justice, obtained promises, stopped the mouths of lions, quenched the power of fire, escaped the edge of the sword, were made strong out of weakness, became mighty in war, put foreign armies to flight. Women received back their dead by resurrection. Some were tortured, refusing to accept release, so that they might rise again to a better life. Others suffered mocking and flogging, and even chains and imprisonment. They were stoned, they were sawn in two, they were killed with the sword. They went about in skins of sheep and goats, destitute, afflicted, mistreated—of whom the world was not worthy—wandering about in deserts and mountains, and in dens and caves of the earth.

Following the path of Wisdom leads to many diverse results, to say the least. In some countries, authorities persecute and kill our fellow believers. In other places, followers of Jesus face intense opposition and intimidation.

Although our ultimate hope of enjoying all the pleasures Wisdom offers lies in eternity, it doesn't nullify the benefits of walking with the Savior before that glorious day arrives. Just as it's wrong to expect health and wealth in exchange for our faith, it's also incorrect to disdain the blessings He brings us in this life or fail to expect visible evidence of His great love as we journey here below.

Please allow me to give an illustration from my own life.

Back in 1991, in the midst of much distress and personal suffering, the Lord caught up with me at the end of a five-mile run. This was fitting, because at the time I was fleeing from Him because of the grievous circumstances I had experienced during the previous six years. As He brought me to realize my efforts to resist His love were futile, I acknowledged my foolishness. "I want what You want for my life," I prayed.

After that moment, I felt closer to Him than I had at any time during the preceding several years. However, after my heartfelt response to Him that day, my life became not better, but increasingly difficult. Accepting Wisdom's call led to additional suffering rather than anything remotely resembling a lavish feast or even a significant improvement in circumstances.

It wasn't until a full twenty years later that I experienced the *beginning* of the blessings that have eventually come my way. After waiting such a long time, I found the love of my life, retired, began a full-time writing ministry, and became an author.

Even so, I know these gifts are but a meager taste of the extravagant blessings ahead in eternity for me, as well as for *all* who belong to Christ.

In our book, *Hereafter*, my co-author Terry James and I explore the many wonders ahead for all New Testament saints after the Rapture of the Church. These blessings will exceed anything we can imagine; even the best outcomes in life here on earth can't begin to compare with the glory that awaits.

Years ago, I sometimes watched a show called "Lifestyles of the Rich and Famous." What's ahead in eternity will be far better than anything featured on that program—and better yet, the blessings will never end.

Don't Settle for Bread and Water

Over the past several years, I've studied Proverbs 9 at least a hundred times. This has given me a growing realization of how the differing paths of Wisdom and Folly correlate to the differing views of God's kingdom espoused in our churches today. Let me explain.

Throughout the history of the Church, the most popular beliefs about the end times have closely resembled Folly's bare necessities rather than the lavish extravagances offered by Wisdom. Why do I make such a daring statement? I say this because the pagan philosopher Plato, with his teaching that all matter is inherently evil, has caused a great many in the Church to deem Wisdom's invitation as carnal, unspiritual, and thus unbiblical.

Augustine (AD 354–430), a highly respected theologian, greatly respected the teachings of Plato. As the result of his adherence to some of beliefs espoused by this pagan philosopher, he wrote that the idea of a Millennium "would not be objectionable" if somehow "the nature of the millennial kingdom was a 'spiritual one' rather than a physical one."[24] He objected to the concept of "carnal banquets," which he imagined to be a part of Jesus' thousand-year reign as recorded in Revelation 20:1–10.[25]

The thinking of Plato and Augustine puts them squarely at odds with the way of Wisdom revealed in Proverbs 9:1–6 as well as what the prophet Isaiah says about the extravagant feast the Lord Himself will prepare for us (Isaiah 25:6–9). Perhaps this early theologian had attended banquets that rapidly deteriorated into revelries of drunkenness and crude behavior, but he made the tragic error of assigning such a debauched outcome to the feasts Jesus will prepare for us in eternity. Augustine doomed the Church to a thousand years of false teaching because he accepted what Plato said about the material world rather than what the Bible reveals about it.

Augustine's errant thinking led him to conclude that the meager offerings of Folly were far more *spiritual* than the lavish feast presented by Wisdom.

Can you see how Augustine's reasons for denying that Jesus would have a thousand-year rule over the nations sprang from human wisdom and *not* from God's Word? Until his time, belief in premillennialism had prevailed in the Church. However, because of his influence, Replacement Theology, or amillennialism, gained predominance.

In chapter 5, we pictured premillennialism as a three-legged stool with the legs supporting it as:

- Words of Scripture
- Jesus' preeminence over all things
- God's Holy Name

In contrast, we might visualize amillennialism as a stool supported by:

- The allegorization of Scripture (assigning symbolic meanings to the texts of Bible prophecy)
- Platonism (belief in Plato's views)
- Anti-Semitism (hostility or prejudice against the Jewish people), which also held a principal place in Augustine's rejection of premillennialism

Sadly, these three "legs" continued to support the amillennial view of the end times until after the Reformation.

Plato's influence remains strong; many believers even today don't fully appreciate the glories waiting in Heaven because they consider physical blessings to be unspiritual, even carnal. When it comes to what they believe about eternity, they settle for bread-and-water teachings rather than what Scripture describes about the wonders ahead.

Isn't it an insult to the Lord to think His promised blessings in eternity are somehow carnal and therefore must symbolize another, "more spiritual," reality? Pastor and author David Jeremiah wrote the following in a devotional titled "Abundantly Good:"

Have you ever heard a sermon about the prodigal soon with the father is described as prodigal? *Prodigal* means "lavish, unrestrained, and unlimited." If you want to see the prodigal in that story, examine the heart of the father who never stopped loving his wayward son.... And who, when his wayward son walked back into the family home, put on a feast to welcome him back. There was nothing that father would not do for his son. That's the way God is. He lavishes Himself upon His people.[26]

The pleasures the Lord will lavish on *all* New Testament saints in eternity will supersede even the best experiences of this life, even those of today's billionaires and celebrities. After we meet Jesus in the air, our joy will exceed all that we can imagine. In contrast to having earthly bodies that get sick and perish, the Lord will give us immortal ones that will never grow old, endure pain, suffer illness, or die.

Contrary to Augustine's unbiblical views regarding the feasts in Jesus' kingdom, we will enjoy tasty food and good wine during times such as the marriage supper of the Lamb (Revelation 19:9). Why should we discount the pleasure of this future occasion when Jesus Himself enjoyed a lengthy wedding celebration early in His ministry on earth (John 2:1–12)?

Don't settle for the bread and water offered by those who deny the glories of what Jesus is now preparing in His Father's house as well as in His future kingdom, where we will reign with Him.

Jesus' Extravagance

Jesus, the personification of Wisdom, exhibited the extravagance of the Proverbs 9 invitation during His earthly ministry.

Consider when Christ fed the multitude of five thousand. After everyone had finished eating, the disciples gathered twelve baskets of leftovers (Matthew 14:13–21). He had provided more than enough to satisfy the hunger of each person in the crowd, which likely far exceeded five thousand, since that just referred to the number of men who were there.

When the Lord turned water into wine at a wedding celebration in Cana, He did so with "six stone water jars…each holding twenty or thirty gallons" (John 2:1–11). Not only was the wine of the finest quality, but the quantity was far more than enough to provide guests for the remainder of the feast. Many months later, the newly married couple was still enjoying His bountiful provision.

In the last recorded miracle of the Gospel of John, Jesus instructed His disciples to put their nets into water one final time. After a night of fruitless toil, they suddenly had 153 fish in their nets—far more than enough to feed Jesus and His seven hungry companions (John 21:1–14).

The Lord's gifts for those who belong to Him are always over-the-top bountiful and marvelous. His steadfast love will never fail. Because of His ample supply of grace, mercy, and love, we need never fear that He will change His mind about us. We remain eternally secure.

The emphasis on the bread and water of this life causes many to overlook the wonderful message of Ephesians 2:4–7, which concludes with a glorious promise concerning our lot in eternity:

> But God, being rich in mercy, because of the great love with which he loved us, even when we were dead in our trespasses, made us alive together with Christ—by grace you have been saved—and raised us up with him and seated us with him in the heavenly places in Christ Jesus, **so that in the coming ages he might show the immeasurable riches of his grace in kindness toward us in Christ Jesus.** (emphasis added)

We see the generosity of our Savior in all that pertains to our salvation and His promises regarding eternity. We will suffer at times during this life, especially as Satan ramps up His opposition to God in preparation for the Tribulation period. But oh, what a glorious day awaits all of us in eternity.

If Jesus' provision for the wedding in Cana was excessive, and it was, just imagine what extravagant bounty He will present at the marriage supper of the Lamb for His very own Bride! What He has to offer will be far more substantial than bread and water.

✑ *Wisdom defends Bible prophecy by:*

1. Teaching us to prioritize the words of the biblical text as our sole source of Wisdom pertaining to future things.
2. Upholding the original intent of the authors of Scripture to whom the Lord revealed His plans for the ages.
3. Magnifying Jesus' Name as the One whose future rule will make possible the defeat of death and the eternal state.
4. Establishing a proper reverence for the words of Scripture, which leads to a deeper understanding of them.
5. Teaching us to fully trust the glorious outcome of our faith when the troubles of this life expose our misplaced trust in outcomes that are often beyond our control.
6. Verifying that Wisdom's extravagant invitation flows from Jesus' great love for us.

Chapter 7

WISDOM LEADS US IN THE WAY OF INSIGHT

Discernment is sorely lacking but much needed among today's Christians. Once-solid Christian colleges, universities, and seminaries are promoting popular courses that teach the Bible through Literary devices. By wrapping their teachings in a winsome and seemingly intellectual style, they cast disparaging shadows across the authority of Scripture.[27]

—Jack Hibbs, *Living in the Daze of Deception*

For many years, I wondered about the placement of the verses between the calls of Wisdom and the "woman Folly." They didn't seem to fit. Why didn't Solomon adjoin the two invitations rather than separate them with the words of Proverbs 9:7–12? Over time, I've come to see how these verses relate to the discernment involved in deciding between the two appeals.

Whoever corrects a scoffer gets himself abuse,
and he who reproves a wicked man incurs injury.
Do not reprove a scoffer, or he will hate you;
reprove a wise man, and he will love you.
Give instruction to a wise man, and he will be still wiser;
teach a righteous man, and he will increase in learning.
The fear of the Lord is the beginning of wisdom,
and the knowledge of the Holy One is insight.

For by me your days will be multiplied,
and years will be added to your life.
If you are wise, you are wise for yourself;
if you scoff, you alone will bear it.

The "wise" and "righteous" already reside in Wisdom's house, as seen by their "fear of the Lord," which provides them with discernment about how they reprove others as well as how they receive correction from others. The scoffers and wicked reflect their decision to stay with Folly, as evidenced by their response to any instruction that might help them return to the way of insight. The simple must choose between Wisdom and Folly based on their acceptance of the sound direction they receive.

Godly wisdom isn't a matter of simply filling our heads with information, but rather filling them with the words of Scripture. It involves living out the biblical understanding we gain over time so we're able to "discern the will of God," what is "good and acceptable and perfect" (Romans 12:1). Most often, this comes as we travel along a bumpy road characterized by conflict, mistakes, and sound instruction in God's Word, by which we are able to distinguish between the paths of Wisdom Folly.

A closer examination of Proverbs 9:7–12 uncovers the key characteristics of what it means to walk in the way of wisdom.

Humbleness

Those who walk in the way of biblical understanding exhibit humility, especially when it comes to the way they handle reproof or instruction in God's Word. Proverbs 9:7–8 defines the differing replies of the "scoffer," a "wicked man," versus that of a "wise man." Some will respond with bad behavior or injurious remarks. The wise, however, aren't only receptive to correction, but they even love those issuing the reproof. Only one of these responses displays any measure of humbleness.

Scoffers exhibit their pride via abusive replies. They refuse to even consider that the advice might be biblically sound or wise. Solomon's concern here goes beyond how one reacts to a fellow believer to that of refusing to humbly submit to the words of Scripture. The Apostle Peter warned of such people in the last days who will mock the "promise" of the Lord's "coming" (2 Peter 3:2–3).

The attitude of those who ridicule our expectation of Jesus' soon appearing often comes from pride that refuses to allow the prophetic texts of the Bible speak for themselves: "'Scoffer' is the name of the arrogant, haughty man who acts with arrogant pride" (Proverbs 21:24).

A harsh reply, whether it's a response to our expectation of meeting Jesus in the air or to our correction of a fellow saint, always reveals a proud spirit. Humility characterizes the way wise people respond to reproof, whether it comes from Scripture or from a friend.

James, the brother of Jesus, wrote about "the meekness of wisdom" (James 3:13). Gifted Bible commentator D. Edmond Hiebert wrote the following about this expression, which I believe fits well with the responses we observe in Proverbs 9:7–12:

> The attractiveness of his life must be established by "his works in the meekness of wisdom." His works, not his words, are the acid test of his wisdom. They must be works of faith, external evidence of God's transforming power within.
>
> The works must be wrought "in meekness of wisdom." The emphasis is on meekness, a characteristic of true wisdom and the opposite of arrogant self-assertiveness (cf. 1:12b). It is that attitude of heart that produces gentleness and mildness in dealing with others—not weakness (Matt. 11:29), but power under control. The meek man does not feel a need to contend for the recognition of his rights or acceptance of his personal views. His life will be characterized by modesty and unobtrusiveness.[28]

Pride always leads people away from the truth of God's Word. This explains, at least in part, why those who mock our faith, whether in regard to the Gospel or to our expectation of Jesus' imminent return, readily reject what seems so clear based upon Scripture.

Abandoning interpretations based on the original intent of the authors of biblical prophecy often comes with an aura of superiority. One pastor roared with laughter as I gave him biblical support for my belief that the Lord will restore a kingdom to Israel. Another responded to my defense of premillennialism by boasting about how the Lord would greatly reward his support of Replacement Theology when he stands before Him at the last day.

I'm not at all claiming to have arrived at the place of humbleness described by Hiebert in the above quote; I have not. However, Proverbs 9:7–12 and James 3:13–18 have helped me use discernment in the way I respond to others' reproof and provided needed understanding of the reactions of others to what I teach them.

The way one responds to a criticism or to the plain sense of God's Word speaks volumes. Those with a humble spirit never seek to demean or harm those who are reproving them, nor do they scorn those seeking to expand their understanding of Scripture so they might better see what lies ahead. The way we handle correction reveals the degree to which the fear of the Lord has produced godly wisdom in us. Notice again the last line of Proverbs 9:8: "Reprove a wise man, and he will love you."

Receptiveness

The meekness of the wise also shows itself in a receptiveness to the reproofs of others, even if they differ from the truth. Proverbs 9:9 shows the positive outcomes for those who carefully consider what others tell them: "Give instruction to a wise man, and he will be still wiser; teach a righteous man, and he will increase in learning."

The wise, or righteous, person reacts positively to reproof or instruction, as we've stated. There's a respect for a fellow believer and consideration for what's said even if it's not accepted in the end or regarded as fact. There's a submissive spirit to Scripture, which opens the door to greater understanding. There's often something we can learn from other viewpoints even if they differ from a biblical perspective of life and future matters.

I've learned much from those who reject what the Bible teaches about the future restoration of Israel and Jesus' imminent appearing. Carefully considering the opposing viewpoints has greatly strengthened my confidence in what I believe. Sermons from an amillennial perspective have

become rich fodder for several of my blog posts and increased my awareness of the weaknesses of the arguments denying Jesus' future reign.

Being receptive to the criticism or even to the mocking of others
doesn't imply that we should remain neutral, make compromises about
our beliefs, or agree with teachings that contradict the Bible. At times, we
must defend the words of Scripture in appropriate ways.

I am thankful for my experiences in churches that rejected me because
of what I believe. It was painful at times, but through the grief, I learned
much more about how Replacement Theology contradicts Scripture. It
has also fueled my passion for defending my belief in premillennialism
and the pre-Tribulation Rapture, which is the purpose of this book.

As believers, we will always encounter criticism; others will at times
rebuke our behavior, our beliefs, or both. However painful it might seem
at the time, the wise humbly receive those words and try to learn from
what comes their way, even if what they hear isn't true or biblically sound.

Insightfulness

Those who walk in wisdom's path exhibit a great perception of God's
character that comes from an ever-expanding understanding of Scripture.
Notice again the words of Proverbs 9:10: "The fear of the Lord is the
beginning of wisdom, and the knowledge of the Holy One is insight."

This verse provides a basic principle for discerning the truth of any
teachings. We must not only assess whether what we hear aligns with the
words of Scripture, but also whether it corresponds to what Scripture
reveals about the Lord. In other words, "knowledge of the Holy One is
insight."

Again, biblical wisdom always agrees with what we read about God
throughout the Bible. Studying the Old Testament is essential because
that's where we learn so much about the Lord and His ways.

For decades, I've based my convictions regarding the Lord's restoration of a glorious kingdom to Israel and Jesus' thousand-year reign over
the nations on the words of Scripture, and I still do. Within the past year
or so, I've come to understand how the attributes of God also confirm my
confidence about these truths.

Each reading of the Psalms gives me a greater understanding of why the Lord must judge the world as described in Revelation chapters 6–18. The popular teaching that says He won't deal with the wicked until the white throne judgment contradicts not only the Bible, but also what it tells us about God.

God loves to reveal the future from "ancient times" (Isaiah 46:8–12), so we should expect to discover much about what lies ahead for the world, and for us, from His Word. And that's exactly what we find. He provided many specific prophecies that Jesus literally fulfilled at His First Advent. Why do so many restrict unfulfilled Bible prophecy to the eternal state and reject what it says about our day?

The Lord gave the ancient Israelites a great many signs so they could recognize their Messiah at His First Appearing. Why shouldn't we expect to find passages in Scripture that speak to His Second Coming? Jesus' assurance to His disciples in the Upper Room still apply today: "And now I have told you before it takes place, so that when it does take place you may believe" (John 14:29).

Just as with the Father, Jesus tells us what's coming not only to increase our faith, but to assure us that He's in control of all things—despite what we currently see.

If we're to walk in the way of Wisdom, we must saturate our minds with Scripture. As our understanding of its words increases, so does our ability to discern truth from error as well as good from evil. Our continuance on this path also rests on our understanding of what the text reveals about the Lord. Our interpretation of God's Word must always align with the "knowledge of the Holy One" that comes from diligent study.

The lack of discernment in today's Church comes from a woeful deficiency in knowing God's Word. Ken Ham, founder and CEO of *Answers in Genesis*, wrote about this matter in an article published on the Harbinger's Daily website:

Biblical illiteracy is at astonishingly high levels in the church. So many Christians don't know their Bibles because they aren't reading them, and they aren't receiving biblical teaching from all of God's Word in their churches. They know a few fuzzy basics and that's about it—and that's dangerous because it's God's Word that changes hearts and minds, that is powerful, and that is our weapon in this spiritual battle we're in. Without God's Word, Christians are weaponless and largely defenseless, unable to effectively live for Christ.[29]

I would add that the severe lack of scriptural understanding among believers has enabled those who teach errant views of Bible prophecy to prosper. Of course, they proclaim beliefs in the inerrancy and inspiration of Scripture, but their approach subverts its words to human wisdom.

Because many in our day fail to walk along the path illuminated by God's Word (see Psalms 119:105), they lead numerous others astray concerning Israel's future and our imminent expectation of meeting Jesus in the air (see Proverbs 10:17).

᜕ Wisdom defends Bible prophecy by:

1. Teaching us to prioritize the words of the biblical text as our sole source of Wisdom pertaining to future things.
2. Upholding the original intent of the authors of Scripture to whom the Lord revealed His plans for the ages.
3. Magnifying Jesus' Name as the One whose future rule will make possible the defeat of death and the eternal state.
4. Establishing a proper reverence for the words of Scripture, which leads to a deeper understanding of them.
5. Teaching us to fully trust the glorious outcome of our faith when the troubles of this life expose our misplaced trust in outcomes that are often beyond our control.
6. Verifying that Wisdom's extravagant invitation flows from Jesus' great love for us.
7. Teaching us the differences between Wisdom's invitation and the cry of the woman Folly.

Section Two

Wisdom's Defense
of Premillennialism

When any vital doctrine of the Word of God has been neglected in discussion and in preaching from the pulpit or has suffered serious and sustained attack but its critics, it is the profound responsibility of those Christians who uphold such a biblical doctrine to reaffirm this truth as strongly as possible. In addition, those who affirm a fundamental doctrine should do all within their power to motivate the church to return to the faith "once delivered to the saints."

One of the greatest of the fundamental doctrines of Christianity—the prophecy about the literal Second Coming of Christ to establish His kingdom—has unfortunately been neglected by many within the body of believers in our generation.[30]

—Grant R. Jeffrey, *Triumphant Return*

Now that we've examined the many ways wisdom defends Bible prophecy, we can move ahead to the specific ways it leads us to belief in premillennialism. Again, this is the teaching that Jesus will return to the earth after a seven-year time of Tribulation on the earth, establish His kingdom, and rule for a thousand years. Today, this perspective includes a gloriously restored Israel, which will be a key part of Christ's millennial rule.

I realize it might seem rather audacious to suggest that biblical wisdom defends these events, but such is the purpose of the upcoming chapters.

Please don't regard what follows as dry theology. The chapters in this section pertain to your future, the glories of which you will someday experience. In chapter 11, we will explore the direct connection between our glorification as justified saints and Israel's eventual restoration as a kingdom. Both result from God's mercy and love, which secures our eternal life as well as the renewal of a kingdom for the Jewish people.

To fully appreciate the lavish feast Wisdom offers, it's necessary to understand why such things lie in our future rather than the bread and water offered by the woman Folly. Amillennialism, the teaching that there is no Rapture, Tribulation period, or millennial reign of Christ, changes the wonders of what the Lord promises into something meager by comparison. The contrast is quite literally between an extravagant banquet inside a beautiful mansion and an offering of bread and water on the street outside the home of a loud and foolish woman. Which would you choose?

As we dig deeper into the matter of biblical wisdom, we see that it defends our beliefs in premillennialism. The words of Scripture, Jesus' preeminence, and God's attributes confirm that the Rapture, the Tribulation period, the return of the Lord's blessings to the nation of Israel, and the millennial reign of Christ lie on the path of wisdom.

We will continue our journey to a better understanding of the feast that awaits us by examining why the Tribulation period must last seven years.

Chapter 8

WHY DO WE BELIEVE IN THE TRIBULATION?

Daniel's prophecy of the Seventy Weeks (Dan. 9:24-27) contributes the most specific chronological information about the future Tribulation by describing it as a remaining seven-year period (Dan. 9:27) out of a total of 490-year time period that concerns Israel. Daniel 9:27 even divides this future seven-year period into halves and predicts the prophetic event, the Abomination of Desolation, which will transpire at the midpoint of this coming seven-year time period.[31]

—Andrew M. Woods, *The Coming Kingdom*

T he third Jewish temple has been in the planning stages for more than three decades. The Temple Institute in Jerusalem has completed all of the furnishings with the exception of the Ark of the Covenant (they claim to know the location of the original one). A few years ago, the institute spent a vast sum of money on architecture plans for the temple, then displayed a video on Facebook of what it will look like.

Israel's government is preparing vital infrastructure to deal with the crowds they anticipate will travel to the temple after its completion. Consider the following from an article on the Israel 365 News website:

> Israel is upgrading its already impressive international airport. The government is also working on a railway infrastructure that will bring international travelers directly from the airport to the Temple Mount. This will enable all 70 nations to come to worship

God in Jerusalem's House of prayer, a vision that the government has already hinted is their true intention.[32]

Are all these recent developments relevant to defending Bible prophecy? Absolutely! Not only does Scripture tell us there will be a temple in Jerusalem, one the coming Antichrist will defile, it also identifies a seven-year period when God will again turn His attention to the Jewish people and Jerusalem. The length of this still-future time comes from the prophet Daniel, who specified seventy weeks of years during which time the Lord will complete His redemptive purposes for choosing Israel:

Seventy weeks are decreed about your people and your holy city, to finish the transgression, to put an end to sin, and to atone for iniquity, to bring in everlasting righteousness, to seal both vision and prophet, and to anoint a most holy place. (Daniel 9:24)

Why am I so confident that the last week of Daniel's prophecy awaits fulfillment? Because the events that mark its beginning and midpoint have not happened in human history.

And he shall make a strong covenant with many for one week, and for half of the week he shall put an end to sacrifice and offering. And on the wing of abominations shall come one who makes desolate, until the decreed end is poured out on the desolator. (Daniel 9:27)

This last seven-year period will begin with a "prince" (9:26) establishing a seven-year peace agreement with Israel. Perhaps the most notable aspect of Daniel's prophecy regarding the seventieth week is the ending of temple sacrifices at its midpoint, which the prophet later refers to as the "abomination that makes desolate" (Daniel 12:11).

Does it make sense that there's a long gap between the sixty-ninth and seventieth weeks of Daniel's prophecy? Yes; the text itself tells us the last week would not immediately follow the cutting off of the Messiah:

> Know therefore and understand that from the going out of the word to restore and build Jerusalem to the coming of an anointed one, a prince, there shall be seven weeks. Then for sixty-two weeks it shall be built again with squares and moat, but in a troubled time. And after the sixty-two weeks, an anointed one shall be cut off and shall have nothing. And the people of the prince who is to come shall destroy the city and the sanctuary. Its end shall come with a flood, and to the end there shall be war. Desolations are decreed. (Daniel 9:25–26)

Several Bible scholars, using the 360-day year of the Jewish calendar, have calculated that the sixty-ninth week ends precisely on the very day Jesus rode into Jerusalem just days before His crucifixion. This fulfilled the prophet's words that after the next to last "week," the Messiah would be "cut off and shall have nothing." Please note that Daniel placed the destruction of Jerusalem and the temple during the interlude between the final weeks. This necessitates a gap of at least forty years before the start of the seventieth week, which we read about in Daniel 9:27.

That leads me to the next question: How do we know the seventieth week of Daniel's prophecy didn't occur in the first century AD or any time since? It's been two thousand years since the end of the sixty-ninth one; is it possible that the last week still remains unfulfilled? Absolutely!

Jesus Placed the Temple Desecration in the Future

About four centuries after the time of Daniel, Antiochus Epiphanes came to power (170 BC). He later desecrated the Second Jewish temple by setting up idols in it and offering pigs upon its altar.

Although the actions of this ancient ruler foreshadowed the words of Daniel 9:27, they didn't fulfill the prophecy. First, Antiochus defiled the temple during the first sixty-nine weeks rather than during the last seven-year period of years in Daniel's prophecy (9:24-27). That alone disqualifies his actions from contention.

Second, two centuries later, Jesus referred to Daniel prophecy of the temple's desecration as a still future event:

So when you see the abomination of desolation spoken of by the prophet Daniel, standing in the holy place (let the reader understand). (Matthew 24:15)

As He answered His disciples' questions pertaining to the end of the age, the Lord referred to the key event of Daniel's seventieth week as a literal and future event; one that would signal the nearness of His Second Coming.

Today, most Bible teachers and pastors claim that Roman General Titus fulfilled the seventieth week of Daniel when he destroyed Jerusalem and the temple in AD 70. However, this is impossible for several reasons:

1. The Lord told Daniel that Titus' siege of Zion would happen between the last two weeks, not during the last one (Daniel 9:26).
2. There's no record whatsoever of a peace agreement between the Roman general and Israel such as will mark the start the seventieth week of Daniel.
3. Daniel tells us the coming "prince" would defile the temple, not destroy it.

Theres also the key detail that the Apostle Paul adds to the fulfillment of Daniel 9:27 and Matthew 24:15—one that eliminates Titus as the person to fulfill Daniel's prophecy of the last week.

Jesus Destroys the Desolator at His Second Coming

Paul identifies the one who will desecrate the temple as the "man of lawlessness," whom we refer to today as Antichrist:

Let no one deceive you in any way. For that day will not come, unless the rebellion comes first, and the man of lawlessness is revealed, the son of destruction, who opposes and exalts himself against every so-called god or object of worship, so that he takes his seat in the temple of God, proclaiming himself to be God. (2 Thessalonians 2:3–4)

The apostle states the coming desolator will blaspheme the Lord, sit in the "temple of God," and "proclaim himself to be God." This is clearly the event Daniel wrote about (Daniel 9:27; 12:11) and Jesus spoke about (Matthew 24:15). There are far too many similarities to dismiss; they speak of the same event.

Paul, writing under the inspiration of the Holy Spirit, adds one essential detail about what will happen to the one who commits Daniel's "abomination of desolation:" *The Lord Jesus Himself will kill him at His Second Coming:* "And then the lawless one will be revealed, whom the Lord Jesus will kill with the breath of his mouth and bring to nothing by the appearance of his coming" (2 Thessalonians 2:8).

At His return to earth, Jesus will destroy the man who fulfills Daniel's prophecy in 9:27. Because the Lord didn't directly kill Titus, nor did the Second Coming occur during the Roman general's lifetime, he couldn't possibly be the one who fulfilled Daniel's prophecy as the desolator of the temple.

Many claim the Lord returned in AD 70 as the Roman general destroyed both the temple and holy city, but this can't possibly be true for three reasons.

First, the descriptions of the Second Coming by those who make such a claim fall light years short of the glories Scripture ascribes to it. Beyond that, church theologians of the second, third, and fourth centuries AD regarded the Second Coming as a still-future event.

Second, in Matthew 24:15–31, Jesus identifies a period of "great tribulation" that will transpire between the desecration of the temple and Jesus' Second Coming, which aligns with the second half of the seventieth week. The identification of Titus as the desolator necessitates that

Jesus would've returned to the earth in approximately AD 73–74, which didn't happen.

Since the desecration of the temple happens at the midpoint of the last week, that means three and a half years, or 1,260 days, must remain until it ends. Daniel 12:11–12 sheds further light on the time:

> And from the time that the regular burnt offering is taken away
> and the abomination that makes desolate is set up, there shall be
> 1,290 days. Blessed is he who waits and arrives at the 1,335 days.

The additional days in the above verses allow for all the events Jesus described in Matthew 24:15–31 with the additional one allowing for the setup of His millennial rule. Just as there's time between the election of a US president and his inauguration, so there will be gap between Jesus' return and the establishment of His rule.

Third, the Lord didn't directly kill Titus in response to his actions as Paul says He will do to the one who desecrates the temple. The Roman General died in 81 AD of natural causes.

John Witnessed the Desolator's Demise

In Revelation 13:6, the Apostle John says the coming beast will open "its mouth to utter blasphemies against God, blaspheming his name and his dwelling." This is the guy of Daniel's prophecy (9:27 and 12:11) as well as the one Jesus referred to in Matthew 24:15; it's also the "man of law-lessness" of 2 Thessalonians 2.

Later in Revelation 13, John states that this same guy will control all the buying and selling throughout the world shortly after he defames God's Name and the temple. This also didn't happen in the first century AD.

In Revelation 19:19–20, John gives an eyewitness account of the destruction of this beast that will desecrate the Jewish temple:

> And I saw the beast and the kings of the earth with their armies
> gathered to make war against him who was sitting on the horse

and against his army. And the beast was captured, and with it the false prophet who in its presence had done the signs by which he deceived those who had received the mark of the beast and those who worshiped its image. These two were thrown alive into the lake of fire that burns with sulfur.

Exactly as Paul prophesied in 2 Thessalonians 2:8, Jesus Himself will destroy the "desolator" of Daniel 9:27 at His Second Coming and then cast him into the lake of fire.

Because a key event in Daniel's seventieth week hasn't yet occurred, we know the entire period awaits fulfillment. Since this is the case, we know God has not rejected His people; His purpose for them and the city, as recorded in Daniel 9:24, remain incomplete.

The Testimony of Irenaeus (AD 130–202)

Irenaeus, a prominent theologian and bishop in Lyons, France, and respected early church father, wrote *Against Heresies* in AD 180 to combat the spread of Gnosticism in the early Church. He was born in Smyrna and received his training in the faith by Polycarp, whom the Apostle John himself discipled.

In *Against Heresies*, Irenaeus wrote:

But when the antichrist shall have devastated all things in this world, he will reign for three years and six months, and sit in the temple in Jerusalem; and then the Lord will come from heaven in the clouds, in the glory of the Father, sending this man and those who follow him into the lake of fire; but bringing in for the righteous times of the kingdom.[33] (Book 5, Chapter 30, Section 4)

This reveals significant details about Irenaeus' beliefs regarding the desecration of a future temple:

- Writing 110 years after Titus destroyed the second temple, Irenaeus believed there would be another temple in Jerusalem.

- Irenaeus stated Antichrist would "sit in the temple in Jerusalem" just as Paul said (2 Thessalonians 2:4).
- Irenaeus predicted Jesus Himself, at His Second Coming, would destroy Antichrist. Isn't this what Paul predicted and John witnessed in Revelation 19:20 as he saw the future?
- Irenaeus thus confirmed both a literal interpretation of Daniel's seventieth week and the words of Revelation 19:11–21.
- Irenaeus also placed Jesus' Second Coming in the future, as did all other theologians during the early centuries of the Church.

Although Irenaeus mistakenly believed God had rejected Israel, he nonetheless asserted there would be a third temple in Jerusalem, which Antichrist would defile. I cannot explain this seeming contradiction, but perhaps the words of Daniel 12:9–13 shed light. There, the prophet predicted that the understanding of his prophecies regarding the last days would greatly increase when the last days arrive, which is now.

Irenaeus' words are not Scripture, but who can deny the significance of the fact that a revered, late-second-century AD theologian believed there would someday be a third temple in Jerusalem in which Antichrist would sit and defile? How can we overlook the ancient theologian's assertion that Jesus would kill the desolator at His still-to-occur Second Coming?

God Is Not Finished with Israel

If the inspiration and inerrancy of Scripture apply to the words written by its many human authors, and that's most certainly the case, then we know God's purposes for Israel and Jerusalem remain intact. We know this because one of the most noteworthy events of the seventieth week of Daniel remains unfulfilled to this day, which signifies that the entire period of the prophet's last week of years must also await fulfillment.

Since the seventy weeks of Daniel's prophecy await completion, this must also apply to the stated purpose of this time, which will reach completion during the last week.

Seventy weeks are decreed about your people and your holy city,
to finish the transgression, to put an end to sin, and to atone for

iniquity, to bring in everlasting righteousness, to seal both vision and prophet, and to anoint a most holy place. (Daniel 9:24)

We know the Lord's purposes for His people (the Israelites) and city (Jerusalem) remain intact not only because the seventieth week hasn't yet occurred, but also because He hasn't yet accomplished all His stated purposes for His "people" and His "holy city." One more period of seven years remains for the Lord to complete all His redemptive purposes for choosing Israel.

If the seventieth week of Daniel still lies ahead, and it does, then it's not possible that the Lord has rejected the nation and replaced it with the Church. Isn't this what the Apostle Paul also clearly stated in Romans 11:1–2?

There Must Be a Seven-Year Tribulation

Jesus' words concerning the yet-future temple in Jerusalem signify that there must be a seven-year Tribulation, during which the Lord will not only pour out His wrath upon the earth, but also bring the Jewish people to repentance. This additionally supports the absence of the Church during this time when Israel again becomes ground zero for the Lord's redemptive agenda for humanity.

Below is a recap of the reasons it isn't possible for Daniel's seventieth week to have occurred yet:

1. Daniel prophesied that during the last week of seventy weeks of years decreed for Israel and Jerusalem, a future prince would defile a future Jewish temple (9:27). He later referred to this event as "the abomination that makes desolate" (12:11). Some claim Antiochus Epiphanes fulfilled this prophecy, but that isn't possible, because he lived during the first sixty-nine weeks.

2. When Jesus gave His disciples the signs of the end of the age and of His return, He referred to "the abomination of desolation spoken of by the prophet Daniel" (Matthew 24:15). The Lord, when discussing the last days with His followers, placed the fulfillment of Daniel's prophecy of the seventieth week in the future.

3. Paul later wrote about the defilement of the temple as a still-future event (2 Thessalonians 2:3–8). He identified the culprit as the "man of lawlessness" and added one key bit of information about his demise. The Lord Himself would kill the desecrator of the temple at "the appearance of his coming" (v. 8). This eliminates Titus from consideration, because the Lord didn't directly kill him, nor did He return to the earth in the general's lifetime.

4. John witnessed the Lord's future destruction of the beast (Revelation 19:20). Writing in approximately AD 95, the apostle's descriptions of the man of lawlessness' activities in terrorizing the Jewish people, as well as all of humankind, for the last half of the Tribulation closely match what Jesus said would happen during this time (Matthew 24:15–22; see also Revelation 13:5–8).

5. Though not Scripture, it's highly significant that in AD 180, prominent early-Church historian Irenaeus wrote about Antichrist's desecration of a still-future temple in Jerusalem. He wrote these words a full 110 years after Titus' destruction of the second temple. At the time, there was no temple in Jerusalem and no nation of Israel to rebuild it.

6. In the previous section, we learned the importance of letting the words of Scripture speak for themselves. When we approach the biblical texts cited in this chapter with a submissive and receptive spirit, we acknowledge that a future remains for Israel. The Bible foretells of a coming seven-year period we refer to as the Tribulation.

❧ Wisdom defends premillennialism by:

1. Confirming that there must be a seven-year period of trouble on the earth, a time of Tribulation, when the Lord will once again turn His attention to Israel and its people.

Chapter 9

INTERVENTION

The day of the Lord follows [the Rapture]. It will be a time when the judgments of God are poured out upon the earth. It includes the descent of the Lord will all His saints to execute judgment on His foes and to take possession of the kingdom…and to reign in righteousness for a thousand years.[34]

—Henry A. Ironside,
Expository Notes on the Epistles of James and Peter

Many Old Testament prophecies concerning the Day of the Lord pose an insurmountable obstacle for those who adhere to Replacement Theology or one of its offshoots. I say this because of the numerous passages in which future fulfillment doesn't require the restoration of a kingdom to Israel. This necessitates that the proponents of this teaching apply symbolic meanings to hundreds of prophecies that could possibly happen apart from a future renewal of the nation. These texts describe with much detail a time of divine intervention in this world; one that has never happened in history.

The claim that God has rejected Israel necessitates allegorizing the Day of the Lord prophecies that describe the coming time of God's wrath upon the earth, the Lord's return to the earth as described in Revelation 19:11–20:4, and His reign over the nations.

This is why premillennialism teachings dominated the Church during its first three hundred years. Even those who believed God had rejected Israel affirmed their unwavering conviction that all John witnessed (Revelation chapters 4–22) were to take place in the future and would happen exactly as he stated. They understood that, regardless of Israel's future, the Day of the Lord prophecies related to a time to come and, as such, affirmed their conviction that the Lord would rule from Jerusalem for one thousand years.

Christian apologist Justin Martyr (AD 100–165) is a prime example of those who strongly believed in a futuristic interpretation of Revelation despite errant views regarding God's restoration of Israel. In his famous *Dialogue with Trypho*, Martyr taught "the premillennial return of Christ and the resurrection of the righteous before the beginning of the thousand-year kingdom."[35]

Below are Martyr's own words concerning the Millennium:

> But I and others, who are right-minded Christians on all points, are assured that there will be a resurrection of the dead, and a thousand years in Jerusalem, which will be built, adorned, and enlarged, [as] the prophets Ezekiel and Isaiah declare…. And further, there was a certain man with us, whose name was John, one of the apostles of Christ, who prophesied, by a revelation that was made to him, that those who believed in our Christ would dwell a thousand years in Jerusalem.[36]

Even if one retrofits Old Testament prophecies to make God's promises for Israel apply to the Church, numerous references to the Day of the Lord remain, including Jesus' eventual rule over all the earth based in Jerusalem. It isn't enough just to reconstruct the passages to speak of Israel's ultimate restoration.

For example, passages as Malachi 4:1–3 don't mention Israel, yet they describe a day that definitely hasn't yet happened:

> For behold, the day is coming, burning like an oven, when all the arrogant and all evildoers will be stubble. The day that is coming shall set them ablaze, says the Lord of hosts, so that it will leave them neither root nor branch. But for you who fear my name, the sun of righteousness shall rise with healing in its wings. You shall go out leaping like calves from the stall. And you shall tread down

the wicked, for they will be ashes under the soles of your feet, on the day when I act, says the Lord of hosts.

These verses stand alone. Even if we substitute the Church for those "who fear my name," how can we place this reference to the Day of Lord anywhere else but in a time to come and include with it a Tribulation period? Those who say it's already happened greatly err because they misconstrue the intent of the prophet.

Let's begin by examining what God's Word says about this coming day.

The All-Inclusive Day of the Lord

If you've ever stayed at an all-inclusive resort, you know that one payment covers the expense of all your food, beverage, and lodging. We discover something similar in the Bible's description of the Day of Lord. It includes many elements that all fit under a single umbrella.

An Extended Time of God's Wrath upon the Earth

A key feature of the Day of the Lord is that it begins with a lengthy time of judgment upon the entire earth. Isaiah 13:6 provides this foreboding introduction: "Behold, the day of the Lord comes, cruel, with wrath and fierce anger, to make the land a desolation."

The Lord makes clear that this time of distress will impact the entire earth, not just the land of Israel:

> I will punish the world for its evil,
> and the wicked for their iniquity;
> I will put an end to the pomp of the arrogant,
> and lay low the pompous pride of the ruthless.
> I will make people more rare than fine gold,
> and mankind than the gold of Ophir.
> Therefore I will make the heavens tremble,
> and the earth will be shaken out of its place,
> at the wrath of the Lord of hosts
> in the day of his fierce anger. (Isaiah 13:11–13)

This will be a time like no other in history. The Lord's wrath will fill the world, leaving in its wake unimaginable desolation and a horrifically high death toll. Isaiah 24 reveals that the terrors of the Day of Lord will not only fall upon all the earth's inhabitants, but upon the earth itself.

Many other references depict this time as one of God's severe judgments of the people of the earth:

Alas for the day! For the day of the Lord is near, and as destruction from the Almighty it comes. (Joel 1:15)

Is not the day of the Lord darkness, and not light, and gloom with no brightness in it? (Amos 5:20)

The great day of the Lord is near,
near and hastening fast;
the sound of the day of the Lord is bitter;
the mighty man cries aloud there.
A day of wrath is that day,
a day of distress and anguish,
a day of ruin and devastation,
a day of darkness and gloom,
a day of clouds and thick darkness. (Zephaniah 1:14–15)

All of these references designate this coming day—one of much death and extended destruction for the entire planet. Doesn't this fit perfectly with what we read in Revelation chapters 6–18, which portray a lengthy time of the Lord's wrath? Both foretell:

1. Enormous death tolls (Isaiah 13:9–13; Matthew 24:22; Revelation 6:7–8, 9:15).
2. Worldwide devastation (Zephaniah 1:14–15, 3:6; 1 Thessalonians 5:3; Revelation 8:1–9:19).
3. A great shaking (Isaiah 24:19–20; Hebrews 12:26–29; Revelation 6:12–14).

4. People terrified to the point that they hide in holes of the ground (Isaiah 2:12–19; Revelation 6:15–17).
5. Signs in the heavens including a darkened sun, moon, and stars (Isaiah 13:10; Joel 2:30; Matthew 24:29–30; Revelation 16:10).

In His discourse regarding the end of the age and the signs of His coming, Jesus warned of this lengthy time of judgment, declaring that the persecution of the Jews would dramatically increase after Antichrist defiles the temple (Matthew 24:15–20). All of this unmistakably links the Tribulation to Daniel's seventieth week, as well as to the Day of the Lord. It's the seven-year period of God's judgment upon the world, which fulfills a key aspect of the Day of the Lord.

Those who say the Lord will not deal with the wicked until the white throne judgment must deny the original intent of the many authors who recorded prophecies stating that the Day of the Lord would include an extended time of wrath upon the earth the wicked must endure before their death.

Jesus' Glorious Return to the Earth

The Day of the Lord includes Jesus' spectacular Second Coming. Notice the similarity between Jesus and the prophet Joel's descriptions of this coming time:

Immediately after the tribulation of those days the sun will be darkened, and the moon will not give its light, and the stars will fall from heaven, and the powers of the heavens will be shaken. Then will appear in heaven the sign of the Son of Man, and then all the tribes of the earth will mourn, and they will see the Son of Man coming on the clouds of heaven with power and great glory. (Matthew 24:29–30)

And I will show wonders in the heavens and on the earth, blood and fire and columns of smoke. The sun shall be turned to darkness, and the moon to blood, before the great and awesome day of the Lord comes. (Joel 2:30–31)

Jesus' Millennial Rule over the Nations

The Day of the Lord is much more than just an extended period of God' judgment; it culminates with Jesus' return to establish His millennial rule over the nations. In Zechariah 14, the prophet provides a progression of events from judgment to the establishment of Christ's rule:

1. The Lord destroys the armies gathered against Jerusalem at His coming, as also described in Revelation 19:19–21 (14:1–2).
2. Christ stands on the Mount of Olives, which causes a dramatic change in geography that provides a way of escape for the Jewish people trapped in Jerusalem (14:4–8).
3. "The Lord will be king over all the earth. On that day, the Lord will be one and his name one" (14:8).
4. The survivors of God's wrath will journey to Jerusalem each year to "keep the Feast of Booths" (14:16–19).
5. The Lord's holiness will prevail throughout Zion (14:20–22).

Zephaniah also concludes his description of the Day of the Lord with Jesus as the "King of Israel" (3:14–20). Verse 20 sums up what the final phase of this time will mean for the descendants of Jacob: "'At that time I will bring you in, at the time when I gather you together; for I will make you renowned and praised among all the peoples of the earth, when I restore your fortunes before your eyes,' says the Lord."

The Day of the Lord is the grand culmination of Bible prophecy, as it features Jesus' destruction of Satan's realm, His Second Coming, and the establishment of His earthly kingdom.

Jesus' Intervention into the World

If I were to sum up the Day of the Lord, I'd say that it marks Jesus' dramatic intervention into the world. Of course, He is active behind the scenes now, as He has been during the entire Church Age. But a time is coming when He will directly engage with our world in an unmistakable way. At first, most will deny that what they see is His direct involvement in human affairs, but by the end, those who remain alive won't be able to dismiss it in such a way.

During his short stay in Athens, Paul spoke of Jesus' coming intrusion into the world:

> The times of ignorance God overlooked, but now he commands all people everywhere to repent, because he has fixed a day on which he will judge the world in righteousness by a man whom he has appointed; and of this he has given assurance to all by raising him from the dead. (Acts 17:30–31)

The signs pertaining to the start of Jesus' judgment upon the world multiply by the day, and we often wonder why we remain earthbound. However, two thousand years ago, the Apostle Paul told us that the timing of the Lord's explicit intrusion into our world was already "fixed."

This coming day, when Jesus makes His presence known throughout the earth, will begin with the Rapture and continue through His millennial reign. In 1 Thessalonians 5:1–3, Paul wrote that the "day of the Lord" would begin with "sudden destruction." Can you imagine the chaos that will ensue after our disappearance? Most people will assign other causes to our departure, but many of those left behind will know what happened and turn to the Lord in saving faith during the Tribulation.

God Must Judge Wickedness in Real Time

Even a cursory look at the Old Testament reveals that God deals with sin in the here and now as well as in eternity. After removing Lot and his family from Sodom, the Lord didn't wait until the end of the age to deal with the sin of the city's inhabitants; He wiped the city out, along with the nearby town of Gomorrah.

God sent Nebuchadnezzar and the Babylonians to contend with the rebellion of ancient Judah. He had to deal with their idolatry and waywardness so He might fulfill His promise to send the Messiah, His Son, to them at a later time.

If Psalm 37:1–20 assures us of anything, it's that the Lord will deal harshly with the evil people who even now are furthering their schemes for death and the enslavement of many under the coming new world order. In Psalm 75:6–8, these chilling words speak to God's intervention in real time to deal with the "wicked of the earth":

> For not from the east or from the west
> and not from the wilderness comes lifting up,
> but it is God who executes judgment,
> putting down one and lifting up another.
> For in the hand of the Lord there is a cup
> with foaming wine, well mixed,
> and he pours out from it,
> and all the wicked of the earth
> shall drain it down to the dregs.

To claim there's no such thing as the Tribulation period not only contradicts the words of Scripture, including most of the book of Revelation, but it also negates God's pattern of administering justice that we see throughout Scripture.

Another key purpose of the Lord's judgment of evil is that it warns others of its consequences. We see this purpose in the words of Revelation 9:20–21:

> The rest of mankind, who were not killed by these plagues, did not
> repent of the works of their hands nor give up worshiping demons
> and idols of gold and silver and bronze and stone and wood, which
> cannot see or hear or walk, nor did they repent of their murders or
> their sorceries or their sexual immorality or their thefts.

One of God's intentions for the seal and trumpet judgments, as described in Revelation chapters 6–9, is to instill a fear of Him into survivors so they will turn away from wickedness and put their trust in Him. Sadly, the overwhelming majority will refuse to repent.

There will be a day when the Lord dramatically makes His presence felt in the world. He's already exercising His sovereignty over human history. Soon, however, everyone on earth will become aware of it—even if they don't believe it.

What Does the Day of the Lord Mean for Me?

Although this topic might seem overly doctrinal and perhaps on the dull side, it has much relevance for our daily lives. I can think of several reasons why this topic is relevant:

God Will Judge the Evil of Our Day

We live during a time of unprecedented evil. Across the world, abortion has claimed the lives of more than one billion innocent babies. Sex trafficking destroys the lives of hundreds of thousands of children each year. Lawlessness, particularly in America, has already surpassed any level that I could ever have imagined possible. Businesses measure their losses from shoplifting in the billions of dollars. Deception and gaslighting have largely replaced truth.

Yes, the promoters of such wickedness will suffer eternal consequences for their behavior (unless they repent and turn to the Savior). The Bible, however, makes it clear the Lord will surely judge the evil that surrounds us in the rapidly approaching Day of the Lord. It will serve as a warning for others to repent lest they also face Hell as their final destination.

As I write this chapter, the world is so close to exhibiting the conditions described in Revelation 6:1–8 that some mistakenly believe we're already there. The Lord's restraining hand is the only reason the Rapture hasn't already occurred, I believe that great event will mark the beginning of the Day of the Lord, which will initiate His dramatic and direct intervention into the affairs of humankind.

We Will Be with Jesus at His Second Coming

Jesus' return to the earth will be the most majestic display of power the world has ever seen. Its glorious brilliance will light up the entire planet, causing people to mourn because of what it means for them (Revelation 1:7). For us as New Testament saints, this isn't just something to study and believe.

We will ride on white horses behind Jesus at His Second Coming. We will have a front-row seat for the most spectacular event in human history (Revelation 19:11–16).

This will be our experience one day. Isn't it thrilling? We will take part in the climax of all human history! Those who dismiss the Day of the Lord as something that happened in the past, or even as something that's occurring now, rob believers of the joyous expectation the Apostle John says will someday be ours.

We Will Reign with Jesus

God's Word also reveals that we will reign with Jesus after we return with Him to the earth (Revelation 2:26–27, 5:9–10). In the book *Hereafter*, Terry James and I describe at length what New Testament saints will experience in eternity, including during the time of Jesus' thousand-year rule.

So not only is the beginning of the Day of the Lord knocking on the world's door, but it is key to what's in store. We're assured that we will miss the Lord's wrath, but will share in His triumph and His thousand-year reign that will also mark this coming time.

We see again how the words of Scripture verify premillennialism, as the prophetic texts not only ascertain that the seventieth week of Daniel remains unfulfilled (chapter 8), but also reveal that the Lord will intervene in our world before He returns.

❧ Wisdom defends premillennialism by:

1. Confirming that there must be a seven-year period of trouble on the earth, a time of Tribulation, when the Lord will once again turn His attention to Israel and its people.
2. Assuring us of the Lord's future and unmistakable intervention in our world.

Chapter 10

GOD'S HOLINESS DEMANDS ISRAEL'S RESTORATION

Our translation for holiness comes from the Hebrew word *qadowsh* which means "to cut." To be holy means to be cut off, or separate, from everything else. It means to be in a class of your own, distinct from anything that has ever existed or will ever exist. *Qadowsh* means a second thing: to be holy means to be entirely morally pure, all the time and in every way possible.

When you put these two elements of holiness together, you're left with only one conclusion: that the Lord of hosts is the sum and definition of what it means to be holy.[37]

—Paul David Tripp, *The Doctrine of Holiness*

I grew up singing the old hymn of faith, "Holy, Holy, Holy," so many times that most of its words remain embedded in my memory. God's holiness remains the subject of much contemporary Christian music, but do we take the time to reflect on what it means?

Until the past several years, I had little understanding of God's holiness. Now, I've come to see that it not only indicates that He's morally pure and totally righteous, but also that He's wholly different from anything we can imagine apart from Scripture. Although God created us in His image (Genesis 1:26–27), many aspects of His being transcend everything we experience or know.

When it comes to God's restoration of a kingdom to Israel, our confidence not only rests in the wisdom we glean from the words recorded in Scripture, but also from "the knowledge of the Holy One" (Proverbs 9:10). This attribute of God confirms that He can't change His mind regarding His promises to His chosen people.

This brings us back to the key theme of this book: What we believe about Bible prophecy must align both with the *words* of Scripture and with what Scripture *reveals about God's character*. We see the latter truth dramatically stated in the passage below:

> Therefore say to the house of Israel, Thus says the Lord God: It is not for your sake, O house of Israel, that I am about to act, but for the sake of my holy name, which you have profaned among the nations to which you came. And I will vindicate the holiness of my great name, which has been profaned among the nations, and which you have profaned among them. And the nations will know that I am the Lord, declares the Lord God, when through you I vindicate my holiness before their eyes. (Ezekiel 36:22–23)

God's character, and in particular His holy nature, guarantees that He must keep His promises to the nation of Israel. The verses from Ezekiel 36 don't say He will act for the benefit of the Jewish people because of their goodness, but rather "for the sake of [God's] holy name." Israel's rejection of their Messiah caused them to lose possession of the land for nineteen hundred years. However, God will fully restore Israel because it's necessary for Him to "vindicate" His "holiness" before the world.

Most of us, if severely offended in such a way, would feel justified in breaking promises, but not God. His holiness demands that He keep His word—no matter what!

In the sections that follow, we'll dive deeper into what God's holy nature means for the future of the Jewish people. We'll see that it demands their future restoration.

God Will Bring Israel Back to the Land

Today, both Palestinians and Jews claim the Holy Land belongs to them. Someday, however, the entire world will know that it indeed belongs to the descendants of Jacob. God gave the land to them, and He will bring them back to it when He fully restores the nation of Israel. Notice the promise of Ezekiel 36:24: "I will take you from the nations and gather you from all the countries and bring you into your own land."

The Lord made this identical pledge to other prophets as He spoke of a future restoration of Israel and a time when they would again exist as united kingdom (see Zephaniah 3:20). Notice the similarity between the words of Jeremiah and the above promise of the prophet Ezekiel:

> Behold, I will gather them from all the countries to which I drove them in my anger and my wrath and in great indignation. I will bring them back to this place, and I will make them dwell in safety. And they shall be my people, and I will be their God. (Jeremiah 32:37)

Many claim that these promises refer to Judah's return to the land after its captivity in Babylon. However, the context of Ezekiel's prophecy makes this viewpoint impossible. In the same context, the Lord reveals that this restoration isn't just for Judah, but for the "tribes of Israel" as well (Ezekiel 37:19).

As further evidence, consider this stunning prophecy regarding who will rule over the regathered nation:

> My servant David shall be king over them, and they shall all have one shepherd. They shall walk in my rules and be careful to obey my statutes. They shall dwell in the land that I gave to my servant Jacob, where your fathers lived. They and their children and their children's children shall dwell there forever, and David my servant shall be their prince forever. (Ezekiel 37:24–25)

Whether one regards this as a reference to a resurrected David or to Jesus as His descendant, the passage still specifies something that hasn't happened since Ezekiel penned these words. Apart from severely misrepresenting the Lord's original intent in the above verses, it's impossible to apply them to the Church or say this has already happened.

The words recorded in Ezekiel 36:22–38 are clear: Israel's title deed to the land depends solely upon the One who gave it to the nation with absolutely no strings attached. God's holy nature demands that He restore it to His people.

Some claim Israel lost its right to the land when its people rejected the Messiah. However, this not only contradicts what the Lord told His prophet regarding the basis for its glorious restoration, but also the words of Psalm 105:7–11, which tell us God's land covenant with Abraham, Isaac, and Jacob is "everlasting."

God Will Miraculously Restore the Land

Note only does the Lord promise to restore the Jewish people to their homeland, but He also goes far beyond that. Notice the astonishing restoration that will take place:

> Thus says the Lord God: On the day that I cleanse you from all your iniquities, I will cause the cities to be inhabited, and the waste places shall be rebuilt. And the land that was desolate shall be tilled, instead of being the desolation that it was in the sight of all who passed by. And they will say, "This land that was desolate has become like the garden of Eden, and the waste and desolate and ruined cities are now fortified and inhabited." Then the nations that are left all around you shall know that I am the Lord; I have rebuilt the ruined places and replanted that which was desolate. I am the Lord; I have spoken, and I will do it. (Ezekiel 36:33–36)

This isn't simply a regathering of the people, it's a commitment to make the land like the "garden of Eden." Since 1948, Israel has transformed a once-desolate field into one teeming with an abundance of fruits and vegetables. However, nothing like this has happened yet.

We know that the bountiful harvests Israel has enjoyed in recent years will end. The continuing warfare in the Middle East, the Tribulation judgments, the invasion of the world's armies leading up to the battle of Armageddon, and the conflict itself will again devastate the land.

At His return, the Lord Jesus will restore all of creation to its original, pristine state, and, under His rule and sovereign protection, the Jewish people will build cities and prosper to a degree exceeding anything they've accomplished before. The "garden of Eden" reference takes this far beyond the experience of modern-day Israel.

God Will Put His Spirit Inside His People

Another reason for placing Ezekiel's prophecy into the future, long, long after Israel's return from Babylonian captivity, is God's promise to put His Holy Spirit inside His people.

> And I will give you a new heart, and a new spirit I will put within you. And I will remove the heart of stone from your flesh and give you a heart of flesh. And I will put my Spirit within you, and cause you to walk in my statutes and be careful to obey my rules. You shall dwell in the land that I gave to your fathers, and you shall be my people, and I will be your God. (Ezekiel 36:25–28).

When the Lord fully restores the kingdom to Israel as He promised through Ezekiel, He will forgive all the sins of His people (see also Isaiah 40:1–2) and place His Spirit inside them (see also Jeremiah 31:31–34). Has this ever happened to the Jewish people? No, it has not. And, according to Jesus, such an indwelling of the Holy Spirit could only take place *after* His ascension back to Heaven (see John 16:7–11). It wasn't until after the Day of Pentecost that we see the Spirit residing inside believers in the way Ezekiel described.

Could this passage refer to the Church in any way? Not if we understand the meaning of the words in the text and interpret them the way the Lord intended when He gave them to His prophet. The words specifically apply to a people who had:

1. Profaned His Holy Name among the nations.
2. Returned to the land after a worldwide dispersion.
3. Received the Holy Spirit's indwelling presence.

Only with much difficulty can one twist the words of Ezekiel to make them apply to anyone but a still-future remnant of the Jewish people.

As New Testament saints, we receive the Holy Spirit at the moment of our regeneration, the time when the Lord washes away all our sins. Other than that, it's clear that nothing else in the passage fits with the Church in even the remotest way. The promise of the Holy Spirit does, however, align with what Paul wrote about the Church sharing in the spiritual blessings promised to Israel ahead of God turning His attention to them after the times of the Gentiles (Romans 11:17–32).

Nowhere in all of the Lord's promises to us as New Testament saints is there any assurance that we will possess the land God gave the Patriarchs. Yet, we find this promise in the same context as that of the indwelling presence of the Holy Spirit.

A Covenant of Peace

Later in the book of Ezekiel, God promised to make a "covenant of peace" with His people, another everlasting agreement (37:26–28). This isn't the one that Israel will make with Antichrist while in a state of unbelief; this one will forever guarantee the security of the people of Israel.

During the past few years, we've witnessed nonstop attacks against Israel and threats to its existence. As warfare escalates, it's easy to see how the nation's leaders might readily accept a peace deal such as the one the man of lawlessness will offer. We know he will break this deal and severely persecute the Jewish people.

When Jesus returns, He will make a far superior deal with His people. His agreement will guarantee their security forever. Will the Lord's covenant of peace end? No. Isaiah also wrote about this pact, and in no uncertain terms he proclaimed it would remain in place forever. Pay close attention to how the Lord's covenant with Noah compares with His promise to Israel after it will have survived the brutal Tribulation:

> This is like the days of Noah to me:
> as I swore that the waters of Noah
> should no more go over the earth,
> so I have sworn that I will not be angry with you,
> and will not rebuke you.
> For the mountains may depart
> and the hills be removed,
> but my steadfast love shall not depart from you,
> and my covenant of peace shall not be removed,"
> says the Lord, who has compassion on you. (Isaiah 54:9–10)

Yes, "we have peace with God through our Lord Jesus Christ" (Romans 5:1). However, the reference here is to Israel. The above words refer exclusively to the descendants of Jacob who will survive Daniel's seventieth week.

The Lord's words to His prophet, as recorded in Ezekiel 36:22–38, validate our belief in Israel's restoration as a nation, the heart of premillennialism. He specifically and unmistakably promises to bring the Jewish people to their land and bless them beyond anything they've previously experienced. He makes the certainty of His resolve to do so dependent upon His holiness rather than upon their behavior. The words of the text and God's character combine to assure us that God is not finished with Israel. He will restore a redeemed remnant of His people to the Land and bless them with a glorious kingdom.

Isn't this what we would expect from our Savior? Don't we see this throughout the New Testament? Our salvation and security depend solely on the Lord, *not* on our behavior. In the next chapter, we'll see how God's mercy guarantees not only the restoration of a kingdom to Israel, but also our place in that realm.

❧ *Wisdom defends premillennialism by:*

1. Confirming that there must be a seven-year period of trouble on the earth, a time of Tribulation, when the Lord will once again turn His attention to Israel and its people.
2. Assuring us of the Lord's future and unmistakable intervention in our world.
3. Joining Israel's future restoration with God's determination to vindicate His Holy Name.

Chapter 11

GOD'S MERCY SECURES ISRAEL'S FUTURE

In words which simply cannot be misunderstood Paul here [Romans 11;12, 15] confesses his belief in a full conversion of Israel, and explains that from it the greatest and most blessed effects will flow out to mankind....

But by this Paul declares not only his belief in a future spiritual and national salvation of Israel, but at the same time shows the significance of this event as including national and upper-national affairs, affecting world history and the history of Salvation.[38]

—Erich Sauer, *The Triumph of the Crucified*

What I'm about to write might seem unlikely at best. How is it possible that a topic unrelated to Bible prophecy could further validate my conviction concerning the Lord's promise to restore a glorious kingdom to Israel?

I'm persuaded that Scripture confirms the nation's continuing place in God's sovereign plan for the future. But several years ago, what I learned as I worked on my master's thesis in seminary led to a deeper understanding of why this must be true.

The title of my paper was "Roman Catholic Justification in the Light of Scripture." My understanding of what Paul wrote about justification by faith, first of all, solidified my belief in eternal security. The message of Romans 8:31–38 is clear: If God pronounces us righteous, it's a done deal. No one can overturn His judicial verdict on our lives.

In other words, it's impossible for justified saints to lose their salvation or walk away from it. *Such things can never happen to those whom God declares forever righteous. Never!*

Long ago, Roman Catholic theologians moved God's justification of the sinner from the time of regeneration to the end of life. I suspect they did this to add uncertainty to the lives of believers, which enabled the Church to exert considerable control over their behavior. Perhaps they understood its finality, and if it happened at the moment that one became born again, absolutely nothing could change one's rock-solid place of favor in God's sight.

Satan's tactics remain the same today; he still seeks to inject insecurity into the final outcome of our faith. He loves to make us feel as though we need to keep earning the Lord's favor rather than believe what the Bible says. He keeps us confused regarding His mercy.

Just as God's holiness tells us there must be a future kingdom for the Jewish people, so does His *kindness.* We are back to Proverbs 9:10 and walking the path of "insight" that comes from "the knowledge of the Holy One."

A biblical understanding of God's mercy confirms the restoration of a future Jewish kingdom.

Paul sums up the vital link between Israel's future and mercy in Romans 11:29: "For the gifts and calling of God are irrevocable."

Please stay with me as I connect the dots between our permanent righteous standing before God and His promise to someday restore a glorious kingdom to Israel.

The Lord Can't Renege on His Promises

As I worked on my thesis about justification by faith, I read a book by Erich Sauer, *The Triumph of the Crucified.* In it, he wrote:

> The question of the Millennial kingdom is therefore not only a question of final history, but touches at the same time the very heart of the gospel (freedom from law, universality of the gospel, gift by grace). To deny it makes either God a liar in relation to

His prophesies or Paul a false witness to us. Romans 9–11 is no mere justifying of God, but a justification of Paul's doctrine of justification.[39]

In Romans chapters 9–11, Paul points to Israel's secure place in God's redemptive program as confirmation that God can't change His mind regarding those He justifies (Romans 8:31–39). The outcome of His promises to us and Israel flows from His character as a promise-keeping God. Human behavior can never negate God's decrees, whether it is on our behalf (justification) or Israel's (the return to the Land and the restoration of a kingdom).

In these chapters, Paul assures us that because God can never renege on His covenants with Israel and David, He will bring all those He declares righteous to glory.

The One who has not rejected Israel (Romans 11:1–25) is the same One who affirms our secure place as justified saints (Romans 8:28–39).

Nothing, not even the nation's rejection of their Messiah in the first century AD, could alter God's love for His chosen people or cancel His oft-repeated statements throughout the Old Testament prophets whereby He gave His solemn word to restore a glorious kingdom to Israel.

This doesn't mean, as some suggest, that all the Jewish people will receive eternal life or secure a place in Jesus' coming kingdom on the earth. Forgiveness of sin and eternal life have always come through faith in Jesus. In the Old Testament, saving faith sprang from believing what God progressively revealed about His Son and His future sacrifice for their sins. Today, we look back with a clear picture of all His death and resurrection signify for our deliverance from the penalty of sin and our receipt of eternal life.

Scripture reveals that the time is coming when a Jewish remnant will turn to Jesus as they recognize Him as their Messiah and Savior. Zechariah wrote about this great repentance of a remnant of the people of Israel, which will happen during the last days (12:10–13:1). Paul certainly had this passage in mind when he confidently predicted the salvation of the Jewish people that would happen after the Church Age (Romans 11:25–36).

Christ also spoke of this future group of redeemed Jews in Matthew 23:37–39. He declared that someday the residents of Jerusalem would greet Him with these words: "Blessed is he who comes in the name of the Lord." They had done so a few days earlier, but He knew many of them would soon cry out for His crucifixion. As Jesus grieved over His beloved city, He found solace by looking ahead to a time when He would hear those same words from a truly repentant Israel.

God's Amazing Mercy

God's continuing mercy toward the nation of Israel despite its past and, might I add, its current state of unbelief and waywardness, speaks to the great depths of His steadfast love for us as New Testament saints. In Romans 11:30–32, the Apostle Paul wrote about God's matchless mercy toward both us and Israel:

> For just as you were at one time disobedient to God but now have received mercy because of their disobedience, so they too have now been disobedient in order that by the mercy shown to you they also may now receive mercy. **For God has consigned all to disobedience, that he may have mercy on all.** (emphasis added)

For Israel, God's mercy signifies that His covenants and promises are "irrevocable" (Romans 11:29). He will not fail to bring the nation to the place of repentance that Zechariah said would happen.

For those of us God declares forever righteous, regardless of our ill-advised behavior, wrong turns, failures, or sins, the words of Ephesians 1:3–14 will always define who we are. Once God justifies us, nothing whatsoever can diminish the unfailing and unending favor we enjoy in His sight.

It's the Lord's incredible compassion that motivates us in our walk with Him, as Paul wrote in Romans 12:1: "I appeal to you therefore, brothers, by the mercies of God, to present your bodies as a living sacrifice, holy and acceptable to God, which is your spiritual worship."

Do you see it? The phrase "mercies of God" is plural. Paul's instructions for Christian living in Romans chapters 12–16 flow from God's unalterable and steadfast love both for us and the nation of Israel. (The chapter break before Romans 12 was applied to the text centuries after Paul wrote to the saints at Rome.)

Our response of service and sacrifice for the Lord flows from the realization that it's not possible for Him to change His mind about those He chooses. We begin our walk with the Lord as those He declares righteous, and we will always remain in His unchanging favor.

In his book, *New Morning Mercies*, American pastor and author Paul David Tripp wrote the following on the message of Lamentations 3:23, "His mercies are new every morning":

> Not only does God lavish on you love that will never cease and grace that will never end, and not only is he great in faithfulness, but the mercy he extends to you and to me is renewed each morning. It is not tired, stale, irrelevant worn out, ill-fitting, yesterday mercy. It is formfitted for the needs of your day. It is sculpted to the shape of the weaknesses, circumstances, and struggles of each and every one of his children.[40]

Is it any wonder that Paul sets our walk as believers in the context of the Lord's astounding mercy that permeates all His dealings with Israel and us?

God's mercy secures Israel's future restoration. Where would we be if that wasn't the case?

Contradictions

The failure to fully understand God's mercy, which lies at the heart of the Gospel, opens the door to at least a couple of inconsistencies in interpreting Scripture.

Many Bible-believing pastors correctly teach the finality of our salvation, yet deny that same unending grace and mercy for the nation of Israel. Isn't it contradictory to proclaim God's unfailing love toward believers, yet deny it for the people God chose so long ago and with whom He made everlasting covenants (i.e., Psalm 105:7–11)?

Don't these ministers see the inseparable link between the finality of our justification and the nation of Israel's fixed and continuing place in God's redemptive program for the future, which Paul asserts in Romans chapters 9–11? Many teachers proclaim the eternal security of the saints, yet tell us that this same attribute of God, His great mercy toward all those He chooses, somehow doesn't apply to the descendants of Jacob. *Such things ought not to be!*

Please note: Paul began his explanation of why God had not rejected Israel after asserting the absolutely unchangeable status of justified saints, which includes all those who are truly regenerated (Romans 5:1; Titus 3:4–7). The nation's unalterable place in God's redemptive program for the future illustrates the security we enjoy in Christ. To teach that God has rejected Israel and replaced it with the Church not only contradicts the clear words of the text (Romans 11:1), but also misses the entire intent of Romans chapters 9–11 as an illustration and demonstration of God's great mercy.

Isn't it equally contradictory for those who preach God's ongoing purposes for Israel to also teach that New Testament saints can lose their salvation or walk away from it?

Those who understand God's irreversible grace for Israel, regardless of its past or current state, greatly go wrong by making our continuing place in God's favor dependent upon our behavior. Our security rests in the Lord's love for us, never in our love for Him.

We don't obey the Lord to gain or stay in His favor. That is something we enjoy every moment of every day and can never lose. We serve Him because of His steadfast love for us.

Paul David Tripp put it this way: "If you obey for a thousand years, you're no more accepted than when you first believed; your acceptance is based on Christ's righteousness and not yours."[41]

There is unspeakable comfort and energizing encouragement in knowing the Lord can never change His mind about us. Such grand assurance flows from His character as a covenant-keeping God who will not fail to keep all His promises to all those He loves, whether it's the nation of Israel or those He has redeemed with His precious blood.

Just as with the nation of Israel, our security in Christ is never about us, it's always about Him and solely because of Him. How can anyone expect that it would be any different for the nation of Israel, which the Lord has pledged to restore?

By Grace through Faith

Jesus endured great agony and died on the cross because no other way existed to pay the penalty for the sins of a lost and condemned humanity. Three days later, He rose from the dead, proving that eternal life resides in Him and no one else.

In John 14:6, Jesus proclaimed that He is "the way, the truth, and the life." No one comes to the Father by any way other than through Jesus and the blood He shed on the cross for the forgiveness of our sins.

Note the simplicity of the Apostle John's words:

And this is the testimony, that God gave us eternal life, and this life is in his Son. Whoever has the Son has life; whoever does not have the Son of God does not have life. (1 John 5:11–12).

If you haven't already done so, please trust Jesus for the forgiveness of your sins and accept the gift of spending eternity with Him. Invite Him into your life. We know that "everyone who calls on the name of the Lord will be saved" (Romans 10:13). The Lord changes us after we receive the gift of saving faith; good works can never transform us (Ephesians 2:8–10).

Call upon the Lord while you have the opportunity to do so; time is running out before the Tribulation begins. Yes, people will turn to Jesus after the Rapture, but there is no guarantee that you will survive the chaos and destruction that will ensue immediately after Jesus takes His Church out of the world.

ᐯᔱ *Wisdom defends premillennialism by:*

1. Confirming that there must be a seven-year period of trouble on the earth, a time of Tribulation, when the Lord will once again turn His attention to Israel and its people.
2. Assuring us of the Lord's future and unmistakable intervention in our world.
3. Joining Israel's future restoration with God's determination to vindicate His Holy Name.
4. Resting Israel's future renewal solely on God's mercy rather than on the behavior of the Jewish people.

Chapter 12

A RABBI, AN ENGLISH THEOLOGIAN, AND ISRAEL

> In 1643, Isaac La Peyrere (1596–1676) published *Du Rappel Des Juifs*, calling all Christians to focus on converting the Jews and aiding them in recovering their land from the Turks.... La Peyrere informed Ben Israel that many Protestants studied the Hebrew Scriptures, believed the Jews were still God's people, and looked forward to the Jews returning to their own land.[42]
>
> —William C. Watson, *Dispensationalism Before Darby*

Premillennialism dominated the early centuries of the Church. It wasn't until the fifth century AD that Augustine steered the Church away from this solid foundation to Replacement Theology, which prevailed for the next thousand years. Although Reformers such as Martin Luther and John Calvin returned the Church to a firm biblical understanding of matters pertaining to the Gospel and justification by faith, they didn't do so in regard to Bible prophecy.

The Reformers did, however, lay the foundation for the Church's later belief in God's intent to restore a kingdom to Israel. Their two principles of Bible interpretation, listed again below for your reference, led to the revival of premillennialism in England and elsewhere in the decades and centuries that followed the Reformation.

1. *Sola Scriptura*: Our beliefs and practices must some solely from the Bible and nowhere else.

2. Scripture interprets Scripture: The clear passages of God's Word must guide us in discerning the meaning of those less clear, because it's impossible for Scripture to contradict itself.

The resulting emphasis on interpreting the Bible according to the intent of the author, accompanied by people having God's Word in their own language, resulted in a great many returning to the belief in Jesus' future thousand-year rule that had remained firmly in place throughout the first three centuries of the Church.

We see evidence of this dramatic shift in the story of how a rabbi profoundly impacted theologians in England during the early 1600s. Who could have imagined that this Jewish leader from long ago could awaken Protestants in Britain to the necessity of Israel reclaiming the land God gave them? *But that's exactly what happened.*

The Story of Rabbi Menasseh ben Israel (1604–1657)

Our story begins after Rabbi Menasseh ben Israel arrived in Holland after fleeing from the terrors of the Spanish Inquisition. Once there, he began forming relationships with English theologians and leading members of Parliament with the purpose of promoting better relations between the Jews and Protestant Christians, which was understandable after his experience with the Catholic Church's persecution of Protestants and Jews.

Even though the authorities did not permit Jewish people to live in England at the time, the Protestant theologians in that country warmly welcomed the rabbi's insights on what the Old Testament taught regarding the restoration of Israel back to the Land.

English theologian Isaac La Peyrere (1596–1676) was one of the English Church leaders who befriended ben Israel. He told him that "many Protestants who studied the Hebrew Scriptures believed the Jews were still God's people, and looked forward to the Jews returning to their own land."[43] (Notice the close link between studying the Old Testament and affirming Israel's right to the Land.)

Menasseh ben Israel later wrote *The Hope of Israel,* which the

Protestants translated into English so believers in their nation could read it. In that book, the rabbi highlighted the "Hebrew prophets' references to a return to their own land, bringing about the coming of the Messiah and a thousand years of world peace."[44] His influence resulted in a "persistent desire" among English believers "to assist Jews in a return to the Promised Land," one that lasted for three hundred years.[45]

Moses Wall, another English Protestant, translated *The Hope of Israel* into English. He wrote these words in the book's preface:

> For the benefit of my country-men who wait for the Redemption of Israel...gathered from their dispersion, and settled in their own Land...surely this Jew shall rise up in judgment against unchristian Christians. ...[who] curse them whom God has blessed. [He called for Christians] to remove our sinful hatred from off that people who are the Promises, and who are beloved for their Fathers sakes; and who are Jews.[46]

Later in his life, ben Israel lived in England for two years. The famous English statesman, Oliver Cromwell, granted ben Israel a state pension of one hundred pounds, but unfortunately, Menasseh died before receiving it.[47] That the most well-known politician of the day would honor him in such a way speaks to the lasting legacy of this rabbi.

What's So Important about ben Israel's Story?

Menasseh ben Israel's story demonstrates how attitudes toward the Jewish people changed dramatically after the Reformation as premillennialism surged among Bible-believing churches throughout England. As the theologians discarded the trappings of Replacement Theology, they changed an entire nation's outlook toward the Jewish people. They saw how the words of the Bible, which they were able to hold in their hands, contradicted those who had adopted the misguided teachings of Augustine regarding the Millennium.

Because of one rabbi's influence and the friendships he formed, England went from forbidding Jews to live within its borders to publishing ben Israel's book in English, honoring him late in his life, and later opening its doors to the Jewish people. The awareness he brought to these English believers prompted many to donate money to help Israel return to its Land.

Because of the foreboding dark veil of Replacement Theology, the belief that God rejected Israel and replaced the nation with the Church, anti-Semitism flourished during the Dark Ages and persisted through the Reformation. Calvin and Luther's hatred for the Jewish people prevented them from applying their principles of biblical interpretation to Bible prophecy.

With the resurgence of premillennialism in England less than a century after their time, love for the Jewish people flourished among the saints.

It's not a coincidence that the current rise of anti-Semitism throughout America has occurred after Replacement Theology took the place of premillennialism as the leading view of Bible-believing churches. The hatred for Jews we see being carried out in many cities is in no small way related to the unbiblical teaching regarding the future of Israel that's taught in the majority of churches today.

The errant message that God had rejected the Jews because of their treatment of the Messiah has again become popular and, along with it, an unwillingness of churches to recognize Israel's claim to the Land. The reluctance of most pastors to defend Israel has opened the door to the resurgence of hatred for the Jewish people that is rapidly growing in the US.

The Resurgence of Premillennialism

After the publication of Menasseh ben Israel's book, *The Hope of Israel*, many theologians and Church leaders throughout seventeenth-century England believed what they read in the Old Testament regarding the restoration of Israel although they didn't possess even the smallest bit of evidence that it would happen or was even possible.

Doesn't the faith of those in early-1600s England testify against folks today who don't believe what Scripture says about Israel's right to the land, even after Israel's miraculous rebirth as a nation and sovereign protection of it since 1948?

Author and church history scholar Dr. William Watson wrote an article called "The Rise of Philo-Semitism and Premillennialism During the Seventeenth and Eighteenth Centuries."[48] In it, he provides much evidence supporting how the generation after the Reformers began trending away from the anti-Semitic and allegorical interpretations of John Calvin and Martin Luther. Dr. Watson lists more than forty-five writers who, from 1585 to 1800, expressed beliefs in some form of Jesus' millennial reign over the nations of the earth.

Perhaps the most well-known premillennialist of the era was Isaac Newton. His study of the books of Daniel and Revelation led him to conclude as early as 1706 that God would again restore Israel as a nation, after which the Jewish people would build a temple that the Antichrist would desecrate at the midpoint of the Tribulation. *Based on the words of Scripture, he predicted Israel's emergence as a nation more than two centuries before it happened.*

I wrote the following on this matter in my book, *The Triumph of the Redeemed*:

> The dominance of premillennialism in Bible-believing churches during the latter part of the nineteenth century and most of the twentieth did not happen because of a few misguided teachers. The roots of this widespread revival of biblical teachings began after the Reformation as students of God's Word applied the Reformers' principles of Bible interpretation to prophetic passages in both the Old and New Testaments and rejected the longstanding amillennialism of church.
>
> The return of many pastors and teachers today to amillennialism, in my mind, signifies a step backward in time as well as a denial of what Scripture teaches regarding a glorious future restoration of Israel. This also signifies a return to allegorical interpretations of prophecy that began as a way to combine Platonism with Scripture and, at a later time in church history, contaminated the purity of the gospel.[49]

Isaac Newton once wrote:

About the times of the End, a body of men will be raised up who will turn their attention to the prophecies, and insist upon their literal interpretation, in the midst of much clamor and opposition.

This day has arrived, but many remain blinded by the false teaching of Replacement Theology. Those of us who insist upon interpreting Bible prophecy according to the intent of the authors at the time they wrote face fierce opposition and ridicule.

ᑫᔐ *Wisdom defends premillennialism by:*

1. Confirming that there must be a seven-year period of trouble on the earth, a time of Tribulation, when the Lord will once again turn His attention to Israel and its people.
2. Assuring us of the Lord's future and unmistakable intervention in our world.
3. Joining Israel's future restoration with God's determination to vindicate His Holy Name.
4. Resting Israel's future renewal solely on God's mercy rather than on the behavior of the Jewish people.
5. Drawing our attention to how the widespread belief in premillennialism during the 1600s sprang from the literal understanding of Scripture championed by the Reformers.

Chapter 13

JESUS' GLORIOUS REIGN OVER THE NATIONS

> The millennial kingdom is not heaven. It is not perfect. But it is ideal. It's an ideal age of euphoria, in which Satan is bound for a thousand years. He is not simply bound by the cross, in that he cannot steal your salvation. No, he is literally bound. Revelation 20:2 says the angel came down with a chain, laid hold of the dragon, that old serpent, the devil, and Satan, and bound him for a thousand years.[50]
>
> —Ed Hindson, *Future Glory*

An online sermon sparked the writing of this chapter. In his message, based on Psalm 2, an associate pastor of a church I previously attended declared that Jesus is now reigning over the nations just as the psalmist described. Such an interpretation springs from the belief that the Church is now God's kingdom, or "an outpost of it," a key component of the thinking that God has rejected Israel and replaced the nation with the Church.

From a wise perspective, such teaching has at least three strikes against it. First, if the words of Scripture matter, and they do, there must be a future seventieth week of Daniel when the Lord again turns His attention to Israel (see chapter 8). Second, as we saw in chapter 9, the Bible is also clear about a coming time of wrath known as the Day of the Lord, which finds its New Testament expression in Matthew 24:3–28 and Revelation chapters 6–18. And third, God's attributes of holiness and mercy necessitate the restoration of a kingdom to Israel rather than its rejection and replacement.

What, you might ask, does this have to do with the assertion that we're now living in the days of Psalm 2? Couldn't we believe in Israel's restoration *and* that today represents the picture of Jesus' reign that we see throughout the Psalms and the Old Testament books of the Prophets?

No, it's not possible. I say this because it's not just the restoration of Israel that demands the thousand-year reign of Christ over the nations, but the very nature of millennial rule that necessitates that we place it in the future, after His Second Coming.

Myriad biblical prophecies pertaining to Jesus' kingdom only find their fulfillment in His future rule over the nations of the earth, during which time He reigns with a rod of iron because of the remaining presence of sin despite the binding of the devil.

Satan Bound for a Thousand Years

The Bible tells us that during the entire Millennium, Satan will be absent from the world. He and his minions will not be able to influence humanity until the very end of this time:

> Then I saw an angel coming down from heaven, holding in his hand the key to the bottomless pit and a great chain. And he seized the dragon, that ancient serpent, who is the devil and Satan, and bound him for a thousand years, and threw him into the pit, and shut it and sealed it over him, so that he might not deceive the nations any longer, until the thousand years were ended. After that he must be released for a little while. (Revelation 20:1–3)

This fact alone indicates that our current day is not the fulfillment of Psalm 2 or many other passages like it. Even a cursory reading of the New Testament reveals that Satan is not bound in any way at the moment. First Peter 5:8 states that the devil currently "prowls about like a roaring lion seeking someone to devour." Other passages also reveal that he is active at this current time (Acts 5:3; 2 Corinthians 2:11, 11:13–15, 12:7; 1 Thessalonians 2:17–18; James 4:7). Paul emphasizes the present activity of our adversary in Ephesians 6:11–12:

Put on the whole armor of God, that you may be able to stand against the schemes of the devil. For we do not wrestle against flesh and blood, but against the rulers, against the authorities, against the cosmic powers over this present darkness, against the spiritual forces of evil in the heavenly places.

Does this sound as though we're living during a time when the devil is unable to attack or influence us? If our adversary were bound in a pit and unable to roam the earth, would we witness the widespread wickedness of our day? No!

Unparalleled Peace

The Bible also indicates that Jesus' rule over the nations will be marked by unparalleled peace—a total absence of war and conflict between nations. Psalms 46 and 47 look ahead to the promised kingdom and tell us the Lord will end all fighting between nations:

Come, behold the works of the Lord,
how he has brought desolations on the earth.
He makes wars cease to the end of the earth;
he breaks the bow and shatters the spear;
he burns the chariots with fire.
"Be still, and know that I am God.
I will be exalted among the nations,
I will be exalted in the earth!" (Psalm 46:8–10)

Psalm 47:1–4 continues the theme of His domination over all the nations of the earth:

Clap your hands, all peoples!
Shout to God with loud songs of joy!
For the Lord, the Most High, is to be feared,
a great king over all the earth.
He subdued peoples under us,

and nations under our feet.

He chose our heritage for us,

the pride of Jacob whom he loves. *Selah*

When the Son inherits the nations of the earth from the Father (Psalm 2:7–12), the kings of the earth will most certainly "serve the Lord with fear." All warfare between the nations will end. This alone shows that the promised kingdom of the Old Testament can't be the Church Age. Peace will characterize His reign until the very end, when Satan stages a short-lived and ill-fated rebellion.

When Jesus truly rules over the earth, warfare between the nations will not exist. Those who say this is the kingdom of Psalms 2, 46, and 110 greatly go astray in this regard. The nonstop wars of our day and of history tell us that Jesus' kingdom has not yet arrived on the earth. When it does, the combined military budgets of all nations will be zero.

A Rod of Iron

Psalm 2:9 says Jesus will rule with a "rod of iron." If this reference is to the Church Age, how is it possible that we would have had all the wars that have taken place since the Day of Pentecost? In the last century, more than one hundred million people have died as a result of warfare and revolutions. Today, it appears that we live on the brink of World War III, which promises devastation and a death toll greater than anything the world has ever seen.

How is it possible that the world would overflow with such wickedness, lawlessness, corruption, and deception if we assume Jesus is ruling in such a way?

This relates to a still-to-come time, which is exactly what we see in the book of Revelation. When Jesus promised the saints at the church in Thyatira a share in His future authority over the nations, He said that such a one "would rule them with a rod of iron" (Revelation 2:26). We also see the future placement of such a rule in John's description of the Lord at His Second Coming:

From his mouth comes a sharp sword with which to strike down the nations, and he will rule them with a rod of iron. He will tread the winepress of the fury of the wrath of God the Almighty. (Revelation 19:15)

If this is what it means for Jesus to assert His authority over the countries of the world, then what we see today is most certainly not His rule with "a rod of iron." And if that is true, then the words of Psalm 2 await fulfillment.

A Restored Creation

Scripture affirms that the Lord will restore creation to its pristine condition at the beginning of His earthly kingdom. He will remove the curse of Genesis 3 from the earth.

In Romans 8:19–23, Paul wrote about that transformation of nature:

For the creation waits with eager longing for the revealing of the sons of God. For the creation was subjected to futility, not willingly, but because of him who subjected it, in hope that the creation itself will be set free from its bondage to corruption and obtain the freedom of the glory of the children of God. For we know that the whole creation has been groaning together in the pains of childbirth until now. And not only the creation, but we ourselves, who have the firstfruits of the Spirit, groan inwardly as we wait eagerly for adoption as sons, the redemption of our bodies.

The judgments of the Tribulation period, as recorded in Revelation chapters 6–18, will devastate the planet, which will require His restoration at the beginning of the Millennium. The prophet Zechariah wrote about changes to the geography of Jerusalem that will happen at Jesus' return (Zechariah 14:4, 8). The verses from Romans 8 point, as stated earlier, to His restoration of all creation to the way it was before Adam and Eve sinned and brought God's curse on it.

In the previous chapter, we looked at Ezekiel's reference to the Messiah restoring Israel's Land to "garden of Eden" conditions (36:35).

As we examine other kingdom passages, we see the impact of the Lord's renovation of all of creation at the start of His reign.

Longevity of Life

It's becoming more common to read about people reaching the age of one hundred. Those who reach this mark, however, rarely live much longer than that, because by then, the aging process has taken a heavy toll on their bodies. It's clear that the end of their lives is near.

During Jesus' kingdom, however, the life spans of the ones who enter the kingdom in their natural bodies, as well as the longevity of their descendants, will greatly increase. According to Isaiah 65:19–20, people will have a much different definition of what it means to grow old during this time:

> No more shall there be in it
> an infant who lives but a few days,
> or an old man who does not fill out his days,
> for the young man shall die a hundred years old,
> and the sinner a hundred years old shall be accursed.
> They shall build houses and inhabit them;
> they shall plant vineyards and eat their fruit.

The words of the prophet describe a time that has not occurred since he wrote them. They can't refer to the eternal state, because no one will die during that time (Revelation 21:4). And there's never been a time during the Church Age when people thought that someone who didn't live beyond one hundred years was a "sinner" because he died *at such an early age*.

The words of the prophecy recorded in Isaiah 65:19–20 point to a time of greatly expanded life spans. If someone dies around the century mark, people will wonder why they perished in their youth. Wow! This is the Millennium and it speaks to the restoration of all creation that will enable such longevity.

There must be a future time when the Lord will restore nature to such a state that people will live hundreds of years, yet some will still die. This can't be the Church Age, nor does it resemble the eternal state when everyone will live forever.

This prophecy points to the time between the Church Age and eternity, which John describes as the Lord's thousand-year rule over the nations. No other period fits with what we read about it.

Peace in the Animal Kingdom

During the Tribulation, "wild beasts of the earth" will contribute to high death toll during the seal judgments (Revelation 6:7–8). But this will all change at the Lord's restoration during the Second Coming. Isaiah 11:6–9 depicts the remarkable peace of this period, when even the fiercest of beasts will no longer be predators, and species that now pose a threat to human life will no longer do so:

> The wolf shall dwell with the lamb,
> and the leopard shall lie down with the young goat,
> and the calf and the lion and the fattened calf together;
> and a little child shall lead them.
> The cow and the bear shall graze;
> their young shall lie down together;
> and the lion shall eat straw like the ox.
> The nursing child shall play over the hole of the cobra,
> and the weaned child shall put his hand on the adder's den.
> They shall not hurt or destroy
> in all my holy mountain;
> for the earth shall be full of the knowledge of the Lord
> as the waters cover the sea.

In other words, the extraordinary peace of Jesus' thousand-year rule over the nations will bring harmony to the animal kingdom as well as to the human population. Isn't this what we would expect in a return of creation to its original condition before the curse? The words of Scripture prophesy of a time characterized by conditions that haven't existed since the Garden of Eden.

Righteousness

When Jesus rules over the nations as described throughout the Old Testament, righteousness and justice will prevail. How could it be any different when "ends of the earth" are the Lord's possession and He rules with a "rod of iron?" (Psalm 2:8–9). Isaiah 32:1 sums up this key characteristic of His rule: "Behold, a king will reign in righteousness, and princes will rule in justice."

When God's kingdom comes to the earth, the rampant lawlessness of our day will soon become a distant memory. The widespread corruption, disinformation, and gaslighting that permeates most governments today will no longer exist under the regime of our Savior who, as God, cannot lie (Titus 1:2). Can you imagine a supreme ruler who never deceives anyone with His words or actions?

When Jesus rules over all the earth, justice will prevail. Along with destroying Satan's kingdom during the Tribulation and with His return to the earth, He will end the great violence and evils of our day. People at this time will fear the Lord as they remember or hear stories about how He wiped out the perpetrators of the great wickedness on earth before and during the seven-year Tribulation.

The words of Psalm 94:20–23 negate any hint of government corruption or widespread wickedness when Jesus dictates conditions in the world.

> Can wicked rulers be allied with you,
> those who frame injustice by statute?
> They band together against the life of the righteous
> and condemn innocent blood to death.
> But the LORD has become my stronghold,
> and my God the rock of my refuge.
> He will bring back on them their iniquity
> and wipe them out for their wickedness;
> the LORD our God will wipe them out.

There's coming a momentous day of justice for those who, by their statutes (and executive orders), "condemn innocent blood to death" via abortion. The globalists of our day plot in vain, for when Jesus, God's King, returns to the earth, He "will wipe them out" and establish His reign of righteousness.

What we see today is most certainly NOT this time as those who adhere to Replacement Theology would have us believe. Satan is most certainly *not* bound, but is exceedingly active in these last days, as seen in his deadly opposition to Israel, his persecution of believers, and in the rampant wickedness and violence that continue to increase exponentially. No, we do not live under Jesus' rule, but someday we will.

Universal Adoration and Worship of the Lord

Whenever I read through the Psalter, I look forward to the time when I reach Psalms 95–100. There I catch a glimpse of the rejoicing and praise that will resound through the earth at Jesus' Second Coming and His subsequent rule over the earth.

Don't let anyone tell you these chapters speak to a spiritual reign; the psalmist is prophesying about God's King who will someday rule over all the nations. The language speaks to a physical kingdom with a visible Ruler who causes people to rejoice.

The words of Psalm 96:9–10 sum up the response:

Worship the LORD in the splendor of holiness;
tremble before him, all the earth!
Say among the nations, "The Lord reigns!
Yes, the world is established; it shall never be moved;
he will judge the peoples with equity."

Kings in ancient times also functioned as the supreme court of the land. So, when the psalmist says God's King "will judge the peoples with equity," he's referring to what Jesus will do in His role as King of the earth. In His regal capacity on the throne of David, Jesus will perform the duties of the Supreme Judge; that's what the above verses tell us.

During this time, praise for our Savior will resound throughout the entire world. It will be a time like no other.

In his lengthy description of the greatness of Jesus' kingdom, the prophet Daniel concluded with the words, "and all dominions shall serve and obey him" (Daniel 7:27). This is in the future, not now.

Jesus Will Rule from Zion

Jesus will reign over the nations from Jerusalem, also referred to as Zion, a location within the city (Zechariah 14:8–21). Where else would we expect to see the "throne of David," upon which He will sit (Isaiah 9:6–7; Luke 1:31–33)?

Psalm 99:2 is just one of many verses in the Psalter that provide the location of Jesus' rule: "The Lord is great in Zion; he is exalted over all the peoples."

Psalm 48:1–3 leaves no room for doubt in this regard:

> Great is the LORD and greatly to be praised
> in the city of our God!
> His holy mountain, beautiful in elevation,
> is the joy of all the earth,
> Mount Zion, in the far north,
> the city of the great King.
> Within her citadels God
> has made himself known as a fortress.

Psalm 132:13–18 conveys the same message:

> For the Lord has chosen Zion;
> he has desired it for his dwelling place:
> "This is my resting place forever;
> here I will dwell, for I have desired it.
> I will abundantly bless her provisions;
> I will satisfy her poor with bread.
> Her priests I will clothe with salvation,

and her saints will shout for joy.
There I will make a horn to sprout for David;
I have prepared a lamp for my anointed.
His enemies I will clothe with shame,
but on him his crown will shine."

Those who claim God has rejected Israel do so in spite of more than one hundred verses pointing to Jerusalem as the seat of Jesus' rule over the nations. Even though Justin Martyr (AD 100–165) believed God had rejected Israel, he still maintained Jerusalem as the headquarters of the Lord's millennial rule.[51]

God's King will surely rule the world from a gloriously restored Israel, and Zion will be not only its capital, but also that of the entire world.

Let the Psalms Speak for Themselves

The psalmists enrich our understanding of what lies for Israel and for us as heirs to the coming kingdom. Every time I read through the book of Psalms, I discover new passages that speak to Jesus' future reign. Why do so many pastors, writers, and teachers assume the prophetic value of Psalm 22, but either dismiss or allegorize the other prophecies concerning the glory of Jesus' kingdom?

Psalm 132:13–18 drips with vivid description of God's fervent love for Zion:

For the Lord has chosen Zion;
he has desired it for his dwelling place:
"This is my resting place forever;
here I will dwell, for I have desired it.
I will abundantly bless her provisions;
I will satisfy her poor with bread.
Her priests I will clothe with salvation,
and her saints will shout for joy.
There I will make a horn to sprout for David;
I have prepared a lamp for my anointed.

His enemies I will clothe with shame,
but on him his crown will shine."

The above words align with all the other references to Jerusalem throughout the Psalms, which firmly dispel the teaching that God has rejected Israel and replaced the nation with the Church. A humble receptiveness to the message of these verses, as well as all the Scriptures cited in the chapter, leads to the conclusion that Jesus must reign as King over the nations when sin and death are still present on the earth. This can't be the Church Age, and it's certainly not the eternal state.

Wisdom tells us to let the Psalms speak for themselves. They can encourage us during the darkest of nights, relieve our fears, and fill our hearts with boundless joy in anticipation of the blessings we will experience when Jesus rules over all of the earth.

The claim that Jesus now reigns over the nations as depicted in Psalm 2 is far more popular than the premillennial viewpoint today, which places it in the future. As such, I have a few questions for those who say Jesus is now ruling as described in this Psalm and others:

1. Does what we see in our world reflect the character of what one would expect from Christ's millennial reign upon the earth?
2. Can we match our current experience in the Church with the wonders the Old Testament prophets ascribed to the future kingdom of God?
3. Is our current experience of a kingdom the one to which the New Testament says we are heirs?

The answer to all these questions is a resounding "NO!" It's not even a close call. It's like the Israelites giving Promised-Land status to the barren wilderness during their years of wandering there.

The writer of Hebrews, commenting on words from Psalm 8, makes this insightful observation:

> Now in putting everything in subjection to him, he left nothing outside his control. At present, we do not yet see everything in subjection to him. (Hebrews 2:8).

There's coming a day when Jesus will rule over all things; nothing will exist outside of His authority and influence. This day had not yet arrived at the time the author (whose identity is not certain) wrote the book of Hebrews, and nothing has changed since. There's most assuredly a day coming when the extent of Jesus' rule will know no bounds.

Please don't dismiss this as a theological discussion with no bearing on your life. The nature of Jesus' rule over the nations has profound implications for us both now and in the future.

The many prophecies related to Jesus' coming rule haven't yet reached fulfillment and describe a time far different than the eternal state. Even if one excludes Israel from the picture, there must be a time when Jesus reigns over the earth as described in Revelation 20:1–10; otherwise, the Bible's prophecies of this time are not true. Of course, once one realizes that the Millennium must happen, it's easy to see how God's promises to restore the kingdom to Israel fit perfectly.

As previously noted, Scripture exalts the Name of Jesus. The prophecies of His future kingdom align perfectly with this as they foretell of a time when all the nations, without exception, will worship Him.

The New Testament states we as the redeemed are heirs to Jesus' kingdom. It matters greatly if our current experience represents our promised inheritance or if a far better fulfillment awaits. It's a big deal!

Wisdom defends premillennialism by:

1. Confirming that there must be a seven-year period of trouble on the earth, a time of Tribulation, when the Lord will once again turn His attention to Israel and its people.
2. Assuring us of the Lord's future and unmistakable intervention in our world.

3. Joining Israel's future restoration with God's determination to vindicate His Holy Name.
4. Resting Israel's future renewal solely on God's mercy rather than on the behavior of the Jewish people.
5. Drawing our attention to how the widespread belief in premillennialism during the 1600s sprang from the literal understanding of Scripture championed by the Reformers.
6. Defining the millennial kingdom as a time of unparalleled peace, righteousness, pristine conditions in nature, human longevity, and universal worship of the Savior.

Chapter 14

PREMILLENNIALISM:
FREQUENTLY ASKED QUESTIONS

What Satan cannot destroy, he seeks to distort or replace. There is a key component of deception with the church today that is often overlooked or ignored entirely: the idea that the church has replaced Israel.

Replacement theology is known by the several names that you have heard of covenant theology, fulfillment theology; expansion theology, and restoration theology, among others. Whatever name it goes by, replacement theology has no scriptural basis and ignores the facts. Be that as it may, well-known progressive pastors and seminary professors are substituting the church for Israel in their interpretation of Scripture....But that is not correct.[52]

—Jack Hibbs, *Living in the Daze of Deception*

My purpose for this section has been to provide a solid biblical basis for premillennialism. Although Replacement Theology and its offshoots are far more popular in churches today, I agree with Jack Hibbs, pastor of Calvary Chapel Chino Hills and noted prophecy speaker and author: The claim that the church has replaced Israel is *deceptive*.[53]

To provide a clearer understanding of why we believe the Lord will someday restore a kingdom to Israel, I will seek to guide you into a basic understanding of premillennialism with the following questions and answers.

Q. What is premillennialism?

A. Those who adhere to the premillennial viewpoint believe Jesus will return to the earth after the seven-year Tribulation to establish His thousand-year reign over the nations of the earth, as John describes in Revelation 20:1–10. The designation comes from our belief that He will return before—"pre"—the Millennium, which is one thousand years. Today, premillennialists believe the Lord will restore a glorious kingdom to Israel during the time He reigns over all the nations.

Q. How does premillennialism align with the three key tests of biblical wisdom?

A. In the introduction, I mentioned three ways that help us discern biblical wisdom and stay on its path. Premillennialism aligns perfectly with these tests.

First, our belief in the restoration of Israel comes from an historical-grammatical method of biblical interpretation of the promises God made to His people. Those who say God has rejected the nation must misconstrue the intent of the authors of Bible prophecy. Numerous passages, written by several different prophets, reveal God's promise to restore a kingdom to Israel. The Apostle Paul clearly stated that God has not rejected Israel. (in Romans 11:1–2)

If we allow the words of Scripture to speak for themselves, they assert that there must be a seventieth week of Daniel, as demonstrated in chapter 8.

Second, a literal understanding of John's words in Revelation 19:1–20:10 align with what Paul wrote about Jesus' preeminence over all things. The book of Revelation exalts the Savior from beginning to end, providing a vivid illustration of the words of Colossians 1:15–20.

Third, premillennialism comports best with God's divine attributes recorded in Scripture. His *holiness* demands that He restore a kingdom for the Jewish people, and His *mercy* guarantees a future for both Israel and us as New Testament saints. We know it's a part of God's nature to reveal the future.

In these three key areas, biblical wisdom confirms the tenets of premillennialism.

PREMILLENNIALISM: FREQUENTLY ASKED QUESTIONS

Q. When did the belief in premillennialism begin?

A. The premillennialism doctrine dominated the first three centuries of Church history. The majority of early Church fathers believed that there would be a literal Tribulation period followed by Jesus' Jerusalem-based rule over the entire earth. Almost all the theologians and Bible scholars of this time held to a literal, futuristic interpretation of the book of Revelation with its depictions of an extended time of judgment, Jesus' glorious return to earth, and His millennial rule.

It wasn't until the fifth century AD that amillennialism, or Replacement Theology, began to dominate the beliefs of the Church. Although this continued through the Reformation, the Reformers' view of Scripture provided the basis for the revival of premillennial beliefs that took place in the decades following.

Q. Did premillennial beliefs always include Israel's restoration?

A. Not always. Although the majority of early Church fathers held to the premillennial view, many believed God had rejected Israel. In spite of this, they believed in a literal fulfillment of the entire book of Revelation, including Jesus' thousand-year rule over the nations. They identified Jerusalem as the place of His throne.

Modern-day premillennialism emerged a century after the Reformation. Although the Reformers held tightly to amillennialism, Bible scholars in the early 1600s began teaching that the Lord would someday restore a kingdom to Israel. Today, along with a futuristic interpretation of the book of Revelation, this teaching includes a belief in the repentance of the Jewish people by the end of the Tribulation and their inclusion as a kingdom during Jesus' millennial rule.

Q. What does God's holiness have to do with the future restoration of Israel?

A. Because God is holy, He must defend His Name against those who would say He doesn't keep His promises or remain true to His covenants. In Ezekiel 36:23, the Lord states He will restore the nation of Israel to a place of prominence among the nations so He might vindicate "the holiness of my great name."

The Lord, through His prophet Ezekiel, clarified that the fulfillment of His promises to Israel rest upon His character, not upon the behavior of the Jewish people.

Q. What does God's mercy have to do with premillennialism?

A. God's mercy tells us His "gifts and the calling...are irrevocable" (Romans 11:29). Paul begins Romans 11 by asserting that God hasn't "rejected his people" and proceeds to combine Israel's security with our own as justified saints. Our perseverance as saints, as well as God's guarantee of a future for the Jewish nation, rests on God's mercy (Romans 11:32). His mercy trumps all human weakness and failure.

God's mercy emphasizes that glory lies ahead for us as well as for the Jewish nation.

Q. What other attribute of God supports premillennialism?

A. Scripture reveals that God loves to predict the future from ancient times (Isaiah 46:8–13). In the context of a warning for the people of Judah, He declares that it's an essential aspect of who He is to tell us what's going to happen before it does. Even when addressing His people as "transgressors," He concludes with a promise of glory for Israel.

Q. How does Gabriel's announcement of Jesus' birth to Mary confirm premillennialism?

A. When Gabriel announced the birth of the Savior to Mary, he revealed that God would give her Son "the throne of his father David" and said He would reign over the "house of Jacob forever (Luke 1:31–33).

The only way Mary could've understood this promise was in the sense of a physical realm with Christ ruling over restored Israel. Like her contemporaries, Mary believed the Messiah would someday reign over a restored kingdom to Israel. Why would the Lord confirm this hope if it was to be something other than a tangible rule over all of Israel?

Q. Is Jesus currently seated on the throne of David?

A. No. The New Testament states that He's now at God's "right hand" (Hebrews 1:3; Colossians 3:1; Acts 7:36). Furthermore, it repeatedly refers to Jesus as the "head of the church," but never as its king.

Q. How does modern-day Israel fit into Bible prophecy?

A. Premillennialists believe the miraculous reestablishment of Israel as a nation in 1948 fulfilled prophecy. It definitely was not a fluke. The prophet Isaiah predicted Israel would again become a nation in a day (66:8), and that's exactly what happened on May 14, 1948, when God, in a supernatural manner, kept His promise to His people.

Some say the current state of Israel can't be the fulfillment of Old Testament prophecies because of the nation's unbelief and waywardness. However, those who say this fail to recognize that this is precisely how the book of Ezekiel pictures the initial reemergence of the nation (37:1–14). The current state of the Jewish people perfectly aligns with what the Bible says will be the case before and at the start of the seven-year Tribulation.

We see this in the progression of the Ezekiel 37 prophecy. The Lord first showed the prophet a valley full of dry bones. Later, He told the prophet, "these bones are the whole house of Israel" (Ezekiel 37:11). Throughout the chapter, there's a progression from dry skeletal remains to resurrected people filled with the Holy Spirit.

Q. Is modern-day Israel necessary for Daniel's seventieth week?

A. Yes. In chapter 8, I provided proof that the last week of years in Daniel's seventy-week prophecy (9:24–27) hasn't yet occurred because a key event scheduled for this time has not yet happened. Since this seven-year period remains for the future, it necessitated the rebirth of Israel, which took place in 1948.

For the last week to reach fulfillment, Israel had to reappear as a nation. Its overall state of unbelief also points to the completion of Daniel's seventieth week. A redeemed Israel would never enter an agreement with Antichrist leading to his defilement of the temple. The current waywardness of the nation, however, makes it vulnerable to enter what one prophet referred to as "a covenant with death" (Isaiah 28:14–18).

Q. Do we see any evidence that Israel might enter such a pact?

A. Yes. Israel's nonstop battles with its enemies amid constant threats of a much larger attack is preparing the leaders of Israel to accept what

Antichrist will someday propose. Even with their recent military success, they might willingly agree to a guarantee of lasting peace.

The last seven US presidents have, at some point during their terms, sought to bring peace to the Middle East. The president of France, Emmanuel Macron, has also expressed great interest in bringing peace to Israel. Vladimir Putin of Russia has stated that a two-state solution is the only road to settling the crisis.

Isn't this what one would expect before the appearance of someone on the world stage with the charisma and power to guarantee peace for Israel? Antichrist will succeed where others have failed and thus will fulfill God's Word.

As I finish up this chapter, more than ninety nations have gathered in Saudi Arabia to resolve the current conflict in the Middle East. The group includes representatives from Israel and the United States. They plan to meet again at the UN in June 2–4, 2025, to continue their effort to draft a seven-to-ten-year peace plan based on a two-state solution, which will divide the Land just as Joel said would happen in the last days (3:1–3).

Will the upcoming meetings of this group that calls itself the Global Alliance lead to Antichrist's seven-year covenant as described in Daniel 9:27? We don't know; however, the fact that the nations of the world are thinking in such a way indicates that we live in the last days.

Q. Is the seven-year Tribulation found in Scripture?

A. Yes! The seven-year duration comes from Daniel's seventieth week. Jesus placed the defilement of the temple during this time, saying that after it happens, the Jewish people will experience the worst persecution in their history (Matthew 24:15–22). John, in the midst of chronicling the judgments of this future event, refers to the blaspheming of the beast, whose reign of terror would last "forty-two months" (Revelation 13:5–6).

John's prophecy regarding the beast, or Antichrist, in Revelation 13 aligns perfectly with the length of Daniel's seventieth week (Daniel 9:27) and Jesus' placement of it during a time of Tribulation on the earth.

Q. What's the connection between the Day of the Lord and the seven-year Tribulation?

A. The Old Testament describes the Day of the Lord as a time of protracted judgment upon the entire earth that leads to Jesus' spectacular return to the earth. It signifies Jesus' intervention in the world as He takes the kingdoms away from Satan and establishes His rule over all.

The Tribulation falls within this time as the period when the world experiences God's outpouring of wrath. The Tribulation begins with the covenant between Antichrist and Israel. I believe the Day of the Lord begins with the Rapture of the Church and the chaos it will bring to the world. At some point after the Rapture, the seven-year period of judgment will begin with the signing of the agreement.

Q. When will the Lord rule over the world with a "rod of iron?"

A. The prophecy that Jesus will someday rule with a "rod of iron" can't possibly refer to the Church Age, nor can it depict life in the eternal state when sin will no longer exist.

We find this prophecy in Psalm 2, which describes Christ's inheritance of the nations from His Father (vv. 7–8). Verse 9 reveals the character His future reign: "You shall break them with a rod of iron and dash them in pieces like a potter's vessel."

Can these verses refer to the Church? Absolutely not! The Apostle Peter refers to Jesus as our "chief Shepherd" (1 Peter 5:4). Jesus "nourishes and cherishes" His Church (Ephesians 5:29); He doesn't rule with a "rod of iron" over His own Body.

Does such a rule fit with what we see in our world today? Not even remotely. The wickedness, lawlessness, deception, and violence shout the message that He's most certainly not in control the way ruling with a "rod of iron" would signify.

The Apostle John tells us that Jesus' rule with a rod of iron will take place at His glorious return to the earth (Revelation 19:14). This must picture His millennial reign, because during the eternal state, sin will no longer exist. There must be a kingdom after Jesus' Second Coming, when rebellion against the Lord still occurs, necessitating such a rule.

Q. How does premillennialism support a belief in the Rapture?

A. The premillennial belief in what the Bible teaches about the Tribulation, the timing of Jesus' return to the earth, and His intermediate kingdom provides the context for regarding the Rapture as a unique event intended exclusively for New Testament saints. Those who adhere to premillennialism disagree about its timing in respect to the Tribulation. Some put it before this time, while others say it will happen in the middle or toward its end. Still others combine it with the Second Coming. In the next section, I explain why the Rapture must happen before this time of God's wrath on the earth begins.

⸂ Wisdom defends premillennialism by:

1. Confirming that there must be a seven-year period of trouble on the earth, a time of Tribulation, when the Lord will once again turn His attention to Israel and its people.
2. Assuring us of the Lord's future and unmistakable intervention in our world.
3. Joining Israel's future restoration with God's determination to vindicate His Holy Name.
4. Resting Israel's future renewal solely on God's mercy rather than on the behavior of the Jewish people.
5. Drawing our attention to how the widespread belief in Premillennialism during the 1600s sprang from the literal understanding of Scripture championed by the Reformers.
6. Defining the millennial kingdom as a time of unparalleled peace, righteousness, pristine conditions in nature, human longevity, and universal worship of the Savior.
7. Validating how premillennialism aligns with the clear intent of Scripture's authors exalts the Savior and God's character.

Wisdom's Case for the Pre-Tribulation Rapture

Here is a message of comfort and encouragement for the believer. Jesus said to the disciples on the last night before He suffered on the cross, "I go to prepare a place for you. And if go and prepare a place for you, I will come again and receive you to Myself; that where I am, there you may be also" (John 14:2-3). That is the promise of the rapture, to "be caught up" as it says in the King James Version. Suddenly we will be snatched away, caught up to be with our Savior.

There are some things we do not know concerning the details, but the big picture of Bible prophecy is clear. One day the Lord is coming for those of us who believe. When the rapture occurs, it will change everything.[54]

—Ed Hindson, *Future Glory*

Now that we've established the biblical necessity of a future time of judgment on the earth, the seven-year Tribulation, we can move forward to the matter of placing the Rapture in respect to this period. It was necessary to establish the tenets of premillennialism because without them, the timing of Jesus' appearance loses all relevance. If there's no seven-year time of judgment, what's the purpose in trying to place the Rapture before, during, or after it?

The arguments in this section for placing the Rapture before the start of the Tribulation period assume a belief in Premillennialism as discussed in the previous chapters. If you believe the next event in Bible prophecy is a distant, end-of-the-age return of Jesus to wrap up human history and the start of the eternal state, my reasoning in the upcoming chapters won't change your thinking regarding the Rapture. They will only make sense to those who accept what God's Word says about Israel, the Day of the Lord, and Jesus' future reign over the nations when people rebel and die.

Please know that what follows is far more than an exercise in dry theology. It's something that affects our daily lives and *all* of our aspirations for the future.

The following questions establish the relevance of studying the placement of the Rapture: Does the Bible teach that the Church will go through the Tribulation with almost all members enduring great suffering and horrific deaths? Could the Rapture happen today, or should we anticipate it happening anytime soon or even during our lifetime? Will believers be alive when it happens?

The answers to these questions will spring from a close examination of what Scripture teaches about the subject. Our opinion of the Rapture, along with its timing, significantly influences the ways we live, plan for the future, and deal with losses that come our way in this vale of tears.

As author and beloved Bible prophecy expert Ed Hindson once said, "When the rapture occurs, it will change everything."[55] I might also add that what we believe about Jesus' appearing also changes everything for us as we wait for it.

As we dive into this controversial topic, we must keep in mind the key aspects of biblical wisdom. What we conclude about the Rapture must:

1. Align with Jesus' preeminence over all things.
2. Fit with the biblical necessity of Daniel's seventieth week. The Bible teaches there will be a seven-year period when the Lord again turns His attention to Israel and the purposes that He has for them and the city of Jerusalem.
3. Uphold the integrity of the words of Scripture according to the intent of the human author.
4. Match the character of God as revealed through Scripture.

With this basis of understanding, we will explore the many arguments supporting the pre-Tribulation Rapture.

Chapter 15

HEIRS TO THE KINGDOM

The New Testament teaching that Israel has been set aside (Matt. 23:37–39) until the restitution of God's dealing with them demands a gap between the last two weeks [of Daniel 9:24–27]. If the seventieth week has been fulfilled, the six promised blessings must likewise have been fulfilled to Israel. None of these have been experienced by the nation. Since the church is not Israel, the church can not be fulfilling them. Inasmuch as God will fulfill that which He promised literally, He must fulfill those things with the nation. It is seen, then, that there must be a gap between their rejection and the consummation of these promises.[56]

—J. Dwight Pentecost, *Things to Come*

To build a compelling case for placing the Rapture before the seven-year Tribulation, we must negate all the popular and yet wholly unbiblical claims that the Church is now the spiritual Israel. Apart from a clear distinction between the two, it isn't possible to defend placing Jesus' appearing before the Day of the Lord descends on the earth.

In chapter 8, we established the biblical certainty of a seven-year Tribulation, when God will again turn His full attention to Israel and His purposes for His chosen people. If the Bible is true, we know the seventieth week of Daniel 9:27 awaits fulfillment because the key event of that week has not yet happened.

What does this have to do with placing the Rapture before the start of the Tribulation? Because if the Church is not Israel, and it isn't, it must be absent from the earth during those seven years. God's purposes for the

145

seventy weeks apply solely to the Jewish people and Jerusalem (see Daniel 9:24). Since the Church didn't exist during the first sixty-nine weeks of the Daniel 9:24–27 prophecy, it's valid to assume the Rapture will happen before the last week.

Author Lee W. Brainard sums up why this supports a pre-Tribulation Rapture:

> If we see that God has returned to Israel and Jerusalem as his program during the Tribulation, THEN we are forced to conclude that the church isn't here on earth during the Tribulation. She has already been taken to heaven in the rapture.[57]

In other words, we occupy a unique place: We're not a kingdom, nor are we an extension of God's promises to Israel. The New Testament verifies the distinctive nature of the Church.

We Are the Body of Christ

The apostles never refer to the Church as a kingdom. In Colossians 1:13, Paul wrote that God "has delivered us from the domain of darkness and transferred us to the kingdom of his beloved Son." Please understand that, even here, the apostle is not equating the Church with the physical expression of this realm, which Scripture reveals will arrive on the earth at a later time (Revelation 20:1–10). In the verse cited above, both "domains" are spiritual. When Jesus redeems us, He doesn't physically move from one realm to another; He will do that when He appears to take us home to glory.

The most popular designation of the Church throughout the New Testament is the "body of Christ" (Romans 7:4; 1 Corinthians 10:16, 12:27; Ephesians 4:12). In eight other instances in the book of Ephesians alone, Paul equates the Church with the Body of Christ (1:23; 2:16; 3:16; 4:4. 12, 16; 5:23, 30).

As such, the Church functions in a way that's radically different from any kingdom. Pay close attention to how Paul describes life as a member of the Body of Christ:

For by the grace given to me I say to everyone among you not to think of himself more highly than he ought to think, but to think with sober judgment, each according to the measure of faith that God has assigned. For as in one body we have many members, and the members do not all have the same function, so we, though many, are one body in Christ, and individually members one of another. Having gifts that differ according to the grace given to us, let us use them: if prophecy, in proportion to our faith; if service, in our serving; the one who teaches, in his teaching; the one who exhorts, in his exhortation; the one who contributes, in generosity; the one who leads, with zeal; the one who does acts of mercy, with cheerfulness. (Romans 12:3–8)

There's equality among *all* the members of the Body. The designation and structure of the Church don't at all resemble any type of dominion with a monarch in charge. Jesus is the "Head" of His Church; He's the "Chief Shepherd" (1 Peter 5:4).

Since He is not now a King who rules over His followers, one would expect to see that reflected in His design for leadership in His body. And that's precisely what the New Testament tells us: It's far, far different than anything we would expect for any type of organization with a ruling structure and layers of governing authority. Jesus' words in Mark 10:42–45 point to a much more unique way of leadership than what we see in the world:

And Jesus called them to him and said to them, "You know that those who are considered rulers of the Gentiles lord it over them, and their great ones exercise authority over them. But it shall not be so among you. But whoever would be great among you must be your servant, and whoever would be first among you must be slave of all. For even the Son of Man came not to be served but to serve, and to give his life as a ransom for many."

In these verses, Jesus asserts that the place of authority in His Church would come through *servant leadership*. Those who would lead must serve rather than use their position to "lord it over" others in their charge.

The Apostle Peter referred to those in leadership positions as "shepherds" operating on behalf of the "Chief Shepherd" (1 Peter 5:1–5). His admonition to the elders in verses 2–3 closely resembles Christ's instructions to future leaders of the Church:

> Shepherd the flock of God that is among you, exercising oversight, not under compulsion, but willingly, as God would have you; not for shameful gain, but eagerly; not domineering over those in your charge, but being examples to the flock.

On the night of His arrest, the Lord gave the future apostles of His Church an object lesson in servant-leadership, one I'm sure they never forgot.

> When he had washed their feet and put on his outer garments and resumed his place, he said to them, "Do you understand what I have done to you? You call me Teacher and Lord, and you are right, for so I am. If I then, your Lord and Teacher, have washed your feet, you also ought to wash one another's feet. For I have given you an example, that you also should do just as I have done to you." (John 13:12–15)

Jesus' pattern for elder leadership in the Church is based on caring for the Body of Christ as a shepherd rather ruling over it. It's far too common, especially in churches that see themselves an extension of God's kingdom on earth, for elders to exert a domineering type of leadership that *silences* the sheep and excludes them from key decisions regarding staffing, doctrinal statements of belief, and building programs.

The equality among believers Paul described in Romans 12:3–8 has disappeared from most of today's places of worship. Far too often, elders and staff see themselves as monarchs rather than servants with leadership roles. When this happens, numbers and money tend to motivate the staff rather than preaching the complete message of God's Word. They sacrifice Bible prophecy on the altar of attendance increases and starting new churches.

The Church is not God's replacement kingdom for Israel, nor is it an outpost of God's kingdom on earth. Such designations arise from false teaching that contradicts what God's Word says about the future of Israel. We are the Body of Christ, not a kingdom.

Many mistake Paul's reference to the "Israel of God" in Galatians 6:16 as evidence of God's rejection of the nation, thus the equating the Body of Christ with the spurned nation. However, an equally valid way of looking at this verse has Paul addressing the Jewish believers at Galatia rather than identifying all the saints there in this way. This view doesn't contradict the many clear passages of Scripture that state God hasn't rejected the Jewish nation.

Isn't this what the Reformers taught with their insistence that Scripture must interpret Scripture? Here, the clearer and unmistakable passages that support Israel's restoration help us understand Galatians 6:16.

We follow this same pattern in regard to the Gospel. I've heard a variety of interpretations pertaining to Jesus' words in Matthew 24:13 where Jesus says, "But the one who endures to the end will be saved." Many use this verse as a reason for adding works to the completion of our salvation both now and during the Tribulation, which can't possibly be true because it contradicts other clear passages of Scripture. The books of Ephesians and Romans negate any rendering of His words that would add works as a requirement for salvation. There, the Apostle Paul makes it clear that good works have nothing whatsoever to do with our salvation, which from beginning to end is solely based on God's grace and mercy (see Ephesians 2:1–10).

We always default to the clearer passages of God's Word.

We Are Heirs to, Not Possessors of, the Kingdom

Those who say the Church is the new Israel make believers current possessors of God's promised kingdom. The New Testament, however, says this is not true. It rather asserts that we're *heirs* to it, such as we see in these passages: Romans 8:17, 1 Corinthians 6:9–10, Ephesians 1:11–14, and Colossians 1:12. These verses reveal that, as New Testament saints, we will one day inherit a glorious realm, which is radically different than saying it's something we now possess.

We see our status as future beneficiaries plainly stated in James 2:5:

> Listen, my beloved brothers, has not God chosen those who are poor in the world to be rich in faith and **heirs of the kingdom**, which he has promised to those who love him? (emphasis added)

It's a great error to identify the Church as the kingdom when Scripture says it's something we will inherit in the future.

As more confirmation that the Church cannot be this promised domain, Paul also states that it's impossible to receive the kingdom in our current, flesh-and-blood bodies. Although this at first sounds like unwelcome news, 1 Corinthians 15:50–53 reveals that it's far better to be current heirs of the kingdom than already living within its domain.

> I tell you this, brothers: **flesh and blood cannot inherit the kingdom of God**, nor does the perishable inherit the imperishable. Behold! I tell you a mystery. We shall not all sleep, but we shall all be changed, in a moment, in the twinkling of an eye, at the last trumpet. For the trumpet will sound, and the dead will be raised imperishable, and we shall be changed. For this perishable body must put on the imperishable, and this mortal body must put on immortality. (emphasis added)

Carefully note that the apostle says it's impossible to inherit the promised kingdom in our current mortal condition with bodies patterned after Adam's (1 Corinthians 15:47–50). The good news is that Jesus will make us fit for this realm when He gives us resurrection bodies just like His when He appears (see also Philippians 3:20–21).

Don't let anyone put a damper on the wonder of your glorious inheritance by saying the Church is the kingdom and Jesus is now reigning over it as a spiritual Israel. Not only does this contradict the many biblical assurances of a restored Israel, but it also radically differs from what Paul plainly reveals about our status as heirs in the *words* of 1 Corinthians 15:47–55.

For now, we serve fellow members of the Body of Christ through the diverse gifts of the Spirit we receive at the time of our regeneration. Those in leadership humbly shepherd the flock over which the Lord places them.

In the millennial kingdom, however, we will rule alongside the Savior (Revelation 2:26–27, 5:9–10). Notice the future reality of Paul's words in 1 Corinthians 6:2: "Or do you not know that the saints will judge the world? And if the world is to be judged by you, are you incompetent to try trivial cases?"

We are not the kingdom—no, no, no! We are *heirs* to it, and someday we will reign with Jesus. But for now, Jesus calls even the leaders of His Church to serve those He places in their charge. He instructs the elders to serve, not dominate or lord it over them.

But Didn't Jesus Say...?

Supporters of the various forms of Replacement Theology point to Matthew 21:43 as proof that Jesus intended to take the kingdom away from His chosen people and give it us: "Therefore I tell you, the kingdom of God will be taken away from you and given to a people producing its fruits."

These words follow the parable of the tenants wherein the Lord depicted Israel's rejection of the prophets, and finally Himself, as the Son (Matthew 21:33–42). Do His words portray the transfer of that kingdom to the Church rather than to a future generation of the Jewish people? No, they do not.

First, Jesus directed His words to the "chief priests and Pharisees," who understood that He was talking about them (Matthew 21:45). Because of their rejection, the Lord withdrew His offer of the kingdom from only the current Jewish leadership. His words don't negate the possibility that future generations of Israelites might be recipients of it; rather, they referred to the Jewish leaders standing in His presence.

Second, decades later, the Apostle Paul asserted directly that God had not rejected Israel (Romans 11:1–2). That clear statement, along with many other promises still in play concerning Israel's future, clarified that Jesus intended His words for the leaders of Israel and not for descendants of the Jewish people.

Third, many prophecies throughout Scripture state the Lord will restore a kingdom to Israel.

We must rely on the clear promises pertaining to Israel to help us understand Jesus' words in Matthew 21:43. Those who stretch His intent to suggest He gave the Church the kingdom originally promised Israel make a serious error not supported by the whole of God's Word.

Many use Jesus' statement that His "kingdom is not of world" (John 18:36) to defend the transfer of Israel's kingdom to the Church. Clearly, there is an unseen, spiritual aspect to His kingdom at the moment. That does not, however, negate the numerous passages of Scripture that indicate this spiritual realm will someday consist of Jesus' physical rule over the nations, with David seated on the throne of David. Nothing in Jesus' words invalidates a future and tangible display of His kingdom.

ᶜᵉ Wisdom defends the pre-Tribulation Rapture by:

1. **Confirming our unique place as the Body of Christ and heirs to His kingdom rather than current possessors of it.**

Chapter 16

THE RAPTURE:
A BIBLICAL EVENT

If you disagree on the timing of the rapture, please don't tell people, "There's never going to be a rapture." No, there must be a rapture or the Bible is not true. There must be a time when the archangel shouts, when the trumpet sounds, and the dead in Christ are raised and the living are caught up (1 Thessalonians 4:13–18). We may differ on the *timing* of the rapture but not the *fact* of the rapture.[58]

—Ed Hindson, *Future Glory*

T he next stop on wisdom's path to defending the pre-Tribulation Rapture is establishing it as an actual event, one that's clearly described on the pages of the New Testament. Those who adhere to one of the variant forms of Replacement Theology claim the Bible never refers to Jesus' appearing for just His Church. An examination of the words of the New Testament, however, reveal that the Rapture is the "blessed hope" Paul wrote about in Titus 2:11–14.

Ed Hindson put it this way:

The truth of the Bible is there *must* be a rapture. There must be a catching up. There must be a time when dead believers are raised, and the living are caught up into the presence of God. If somebody doesn't believe in the pretribulation rapture, they should not go around saying, "Well, I don't believe there is ever going to be a rapture." They simply don't agree with the *timing* of the event.

The fact of the rapture is clear in the Bible. If you say you don't believe in the rapture, you don't believe the Bible. You might as well rip 1 Thessalonians 4 out of the Bible and throw it away. It's the whole basis of the believer's blessed hope (Titus 3:13).[59]

In other words, *the Bible supports our anticipation of meeting Jesus in the air.* Those who say there's no such thing as the Rapture can't justify such a statement because it contradicts the clear intent of many New Testament passages.

The Event We Call the Rapture

The word "rapture" comes from a Latin translation of the Bible called the Vulgate, which dates from about AD 400. The Latin word *rapturo* appears in 1 Thessalonians 4:17 as the translation of the Greek word *harpazo*. The words "caught up" in our English versions of this verse capture the essence of the Greek *harpazo*, just as the Latin *rapturo* did when Jerome and others translated the Bible into Latin.

Joseph Mede (1586–1639), an English Bible scholar who lived shortly after the Reformation, used the word "rapture" six times in a letter he wrote in 1627. He used the word in reference "to the saints meeting Jesus in the air" as described in 1 Thessalonians 4:17:[60] "Although Mede seemed to suggest a post-tribulation rapture, he allowed for a bit of time between the rapture and the return to earth of the saints."[61] Please note that Mede used the word "rapture" the same way we do today. He did that *four centuries ago* and *more than two hundred years before the time of John Darby, whom many claim originated the concept of the Rapture.* They say no one believed in the early removal of the Church from the earth before his day.

In his book *Dispensationalism Before Darby*, Dr. William C. Watson lists ten instances of Bible scholars using the word the word "Rapture" to refer to Jesus' appearing; he cites examples of this beginning with Joseph Mede in 1627 through the time of Thomas Broughton, an English pastor, in 1768.[62] In the centuries after the Reformation, the usage of the word

"Rapture" to describe the event depicted in 1 Thessalonians 4:14–17, quoted below, became commonplace among biblical commentators and researchers:

> For since we believe that Jesus died and rose again, even so, through Jesus, God will bring with him those who have fallen asleep. For this we declare to you by a word from the Lord, that we who are alive, who are left until the coming of the Lord, will not precede those who have fallen asleep. For the Lord himself will descend from heaven with a cry of command, with the voice of an archangel, and with the sound of the trumpet of God. And the dead in Christ will rise first. Then we who are alive, who are left, will be caught up together with them in the clouds to meet the Lord in the air, and so we will always be with the Lord. Therefore encourage one another with these words.

We find additional depictions of this event in John 14:2–3, 1 Corinthians 15:50–55, Philippians 3:20–21, Romans 8:23–25, Titus 2:11–14, and Colossians 3:4. Putting these passages together, we have the following sequence (that also appears in my earlier-mentioned book, *Hereafter*, which I coauthored with Terry James):

1. Jesus descends from Heaven (1 Thessalonians 4:16).
2. There's a cry of command, along with the shout of the archangel (1 Thessalonians 4:16).
3. The trumpet of God sounds (1 Thessalonians 4:16).
4. Jesus first raises the dead in Christ with immortal bodies, and He joins them to the souls He brings with Him (1 Thessalonians 4:14–16; 1 Corinthians 15:52).
5. In the "twinkling of an eye," believers who are alive receive their immortal bodies and meet Jesus in the air (1 Thessalonians 4:17; 1 Corinthians 15:50–54; Philippians 3:20–21; Romans 8:23–25).

6. Jesus takes His Bride, the Church, to the place He's prepared for them in His Father's house (John 14:2–3, 17:24).
7. We appear with Jesus in glory (Colossians 3:4).[63]

This definitely is "not a fictional belief based on mysterious visions from the nineteenth century or the sole invention of John Darby as many claim," Terry and I noted in our book. "No, it's a term that Bible students apply to the sequence of events described in the references cited above."[64]

Harpazo is the word Paul used to describe Jesus taking us up by force away from the earth to meet Him in the air. In Romans 8:23–24, Paul refers to this event as the "redemption of our bodies," then states, "For in this hope we were saved." This is the hope embedded in the gospel message.

Our Receipt of Immortal Bodies

Based on the biblical depictions of Jesus' appearing, we learn that this is when He gives us immortal and imperishable bodies. As noted in the previous chapter, there must be a time when the words of 1 Corinthians 15:50–53 reach fulfillment:

> I tell you this, brothers: flesh and blood cannot inherit the kingdom of God, nor does the perishable inherit the imperishable. Behold! I tell you a mystery. We shall not all sleep, but we shall all be changed, in a moment, in the twinkling of an eye, at the last trumpet. For the trumpet will sound, and the dead will be raised imperishable, and we shall be changed. For this perishable body must put on the imperishable, and this mortal body must put on immortality.

These verses describe the Rapture and represent another reason for affirming it as a biblical necessity. Regardless of where we place this event in proximity to the Tribulation, it must happen. If the Bible is true, there must be a time when Jesus raises the dead in Christ from their graves and instantly transforms us, the living saints.

Some writers and pastors say the promise of the above passage happens at the moment of our regeneration. They say the apostle is referring to a past event in the life of the believer rather than a future expectation. Did you know Paul confronted this same error shortly before his death?

> Among them are Hymenaeus and Philetus, who have swerved from the truth, saying that the resurrection has already happened. They are upsetting the faith of some. (2 Timothy 2:17b–18)

The future resurrection of believers, the dominant theme of 1 Corinthian 15, is our "blessed hope." Those today who place our receipt of resurrection and immortal bodies in the past are repeating the identical false teaching of Hymenaeus and Philetus, and, just like this pair, severely harm members of the Body of Christ.

Even among churches that place our receipt of incorruptible bodies in a day yet to come, there's a remarkable silence regarding this hope. It's not uncommon today to hear presentations of the gospel without one mention of the words "eternal life."

There's an old expression that dates back to 1512: "Throwing out the baby with bath water." The idea behind the saying is that if you believe part of an idea or teaching is not good, don't toss it all away.

Isn't this what many pastors do today? They fear the negative results of mentioning the dreaded "R" word—"Rapture"—from the pulpit. As the result of refusing to acknowledge any aspect of Jesus' future appearing, they never speak of the resurrection of the dead in Christ or the glorious transformation of those who will be alive at the time. *Water and baby both go out the window.*

The words of Scripture guarantee we will live forever in imperishable bodies like that of our Lord Jesus, but sadly, it's one of the most frequently neglected biblical truths.

The words of 1 Corinthians 15:19 sum up the necessity of our hope of immortality: "If in Christ we have hope in this life only, we are of all people most to be pitied."

In the verses leading up to this one, Paul refutes the argument of those in Corinth who claimed there was no such thing as a resurrection (15:12–18). If true, he argues, then we must conclude that Jesus didn't rise from the dead, which would deem our faith "futile." The end of such a dire possibility is that the "dead in Christ" have perished, and we who are alive are "most to be pitied" (ESV) or "miserable" (KJV) because our hope doesn't extend beyond this life (see vv. 18–19).

Paul begins verse 1 Corinthians 15:20 with the glorious fact that "Christ has been raised from the dead," and in 1 Corinthians 15:47–57, he sums up our forever hope with the joyous reality of our bodily resurrection as New Testament saints. In language that others cannot possibly misconstrue or misunderstand, the apostle says a time is coming when Jesus will raise the dead with imperishable bodies and gloriously transform believers still alive at His appearing, the Rapture of His Church.

Paul again wrote about our jubilant hope in Philippians 3:20–21: "But our citizenship is in heaven, and from it we await a Savior, the Lord Jesus Christ, **who will transform our lowly body to be like his glorious body**, by the power that enables him even to subject all things to himself" (emphasis added).

Because Jesus rose from the dead, our hope is that someday we will possess a glorious body like that of our Savior. The sense of verse 20 is an excited anticipation of Jesus' appearing. It signifies a yearning of soul for the time when Jesus will raise the dead in Christ and wholly transform us with immortality.

If you are a pastor or teacher, please don't further perpetuate the injurious error of Hymenaeus and Philetus by never talking about the wondrous promise of receiving resurrection and immortal bodies at the time of Jesus' appearing (1 Corinthians 15:47–55).

The Testimony of Church History

As I documented in my book, *The Triumph of the Redeemed*, premillennialism was embedded in the Church during its first three hundred years. The early theologians viewed the book of Revelation as a literal depiction of a time of trials on the earth followed by Jesus' glorious Second Coming and His establishment of a thousand-year reign over the nations.

There's also considerable evidence that many in the early centuries of Christendom believed Jesus would take His saints to Heaven, followed by a time of tribulation on the earth. Though the idea of pre-Tribulation Rapture wouldn't come into focus until much later, many Bible students placed Tribulation on the earth between Jesus appearing to take His saints out of the world and His Second Coming.

Irenaeus, the prominent bishop mentioned earlier, who in AD 180 authored *Against Heresies* to refute the errors of Gnosticism, wrote in his famous work: "And therefore, when in the end the Church shall be suddenly caught up from this, it is said, "There shall be Tribulation such as has not been since the beginning, neither shall be."[65] (Book 5, Chapter 29)

Irenaeus asserted a clear belief in a Tribulation that would take place after Jesus "caught up" His Church out of the world. He used the same Greek word, *harpazo*, that Paul used in 1 Thessalonians 4:17 for the Lord catching up living believers to meet Him in the air. It's also noteworthy to point out that this respected theologian placed the *harpazo* before the time of "great tribulation," which Jesus said would follow the desecration of the temple (Matthew 24:15–21).

We find a similar belief in the writing of Cyprian, a bishop in the city of Carthage during the third century AD, who guided his church through intense persecution and suffering.

In his book, *Treatises of Cyprian,* he wrote:

We who see that terrible things have begun, and know that still more terrible things are imminent, may regard it as the greatest advantage to depart from it as quickly as possible. Do you not give God thanks, do you not congratulate yourself, that by an early departure you are taken away, and delivered from the shipwrecks and disasters that are imminent? Let us greet the day which assigns each of us to his own home, which snatches us hence, and sets us free from the snares of the world and restores us to paradise and the kingdom.[66]

Similar to the beliefs of Irenaeus, Cyprian believed Jesus would remove His Church from the earth before a time of "disasters" on the earth. He wrote that a period of additional trouble was "imminent," and by means of an "early departure," Jesus would take believers away so they wouldn't experience the suffering that would follow.

Cyprian's description of our "departure" sounds quite similar to what many refer to today as the pre-Tribulation Rapture. It's clear that both he and Irenaeus believed Jesus would take His Church to Heaven before God's wrath would fall upon the earth. Both clearly adhered to a literal, futuristic interpretation of the book of Revelation.

Many other quotes from writers during the early centuries of the Church also express beliefs in the Church's departure before God's judgment.

It would be a stretch to attempt to categorize all the references to the exit of the Church in the early seven centuries of the Church as referring to a pre-Tribulation Rapture. However, they can be summed up by stating they convey a clear separation of time between the Rapture and the Second Coming. None of the early biblical scholars identify the return of Jesus for His Church with the Second Coming.

Wisdom defends the pre-Tribulation Rapture by:

1. Confirming our unique place as the Body of Christ and heirs to His kingdom rather than current possessors of it.
2. Verifying that the Rapture, as described in 1 Thessalonians 4:13–17, must happen if the Bible is true.

Chapter 17

ONE IS NOT
LIKE THE OTHER

The pretribulation rapture involves Christ coming *for* His saints in the air before the tribulation, whereas at the second coming He will come back *with* His saints to the earth to reign for 1,000 years (Revelation 19; 20:1–6). The fact that Christ comes "with" His "holy ones" (redeemed believers) at the second coming presumes they have been previously raptured. In other words, Christ cannot come from heaven to earth *with* them (at the second coming) until He has first come to earth *for* them (at the rapture).[67]

—Ron Rhodes, *Bible Prophecy Under Siege*

In our efforts to place the Rapture before the Tribulation period, the next step is to separate it from Christ's Second Coming. We saw this pattern in the writings of early Church leaders, but now we must make this distinction based on the words of Scripture.

Those who combine these two events reside in two differing camps. The first group consists of those who hold to Replacement Theology. They either deny that there is a Rapture or combine it with the Second Coming at the end of age.

Some who believe in a literal, seven-year Tribulation also merge the events. They believe in a post-Tribulation Rapture, in which Jesus catches up His saints when He returns to earth to initiate His millennial reign as described in Revelation 19:11–20:4. These insist that the Church will endure the coming time of wrath with Jesus taking His saints out of the world as part of His return to it. In other words, He catches us up to greet Him as He descends to the earth.

Understanding the differences between the Rapture and Second Coming assumes the following points we established in the previous chapters:

1. Biblical wisdom comes to us exclusively through the *words* of Scripture.
2. Israel and the Church are two distinct entities. Though both Jews and Gentiles are now a part of the Body of Christ, the Lord will again turn His attention to completing His purposes for the Jewish people and Jerusalem during the remaining seventieth week of Daniel.
3. The Rapture is a biblical event described in several New Testament passages.

Based on these sound assumptions, we will examine the evidence not only for distinguishing Jesus appearing for His Church from His Second Coming, but also for the need to separate them with a significant amount of time.

Timing of the Resurrection of the Dead

When Jesus appears to take us to glory, He will immediately raise the "dead in Christ," as Paul writes in 1 Thessalonians 4:15–16:

> For this we declare to you by a word from the Lord, that we who are alive, who are left until the coming of the Lord, will not precede those who have fallen asleep. For the Lord himself will descend from heaven with a cry of command, with the voice of an archangel, and with the sound of the trumpet of God. And the dead in Christ will rise first.

Please note the emphasis with which the apostle reveals that at His appearing, Jesus will "*first*" resurrect those who died as believers in Christ for salvation. Paul affirms, via a direct "word from the Lord," that "the dead in Christ will rise first." We see this exact order of events presented in 1 Corinthians 15:51–53.

With the Second Coming, we see an entirely different sequence of events. God's Word reveals that many things will occur *before* Jesus raises the Tribulation saints from the dead. Here is all the Lord will accomplish beforehand:

1. All the people of the earth will witness His coming in the clouds (Revelation 1:7; Matthew 24:30).
2. His feet will touch down on the Mount of Olives (Zechariah 14:4).
3. He will fight against the armies gathered against Jerusalem (Zechariah 14:1–4).
4. He will cause an earthquake enabling those in the city to escape (Zechariah 14:1–4).
5. He will capture and destroy Antichrist and the False Prophet (Revelation 19:20).
6. An angel will bind Satan, throw him into a pit, and seal it so he is no longer able to "deceive the nations" (Revelation 20:1–4).
7. Thrones appear, with those seated upon them possessing "authority to judge" (Revelation 20:4).

At a minimum, several hours will transpire between the time Jesus first appears in the clouds at His Second Coming and the resurrection of the dead Tribulation saints. It's conceivable that He will raise those believers several days later. It's something that happens *after* His return to earth rather than as a part of it.

By itself, the placement of the resurrections convinces me that it's not possible to combine the Rapture and Second Coming, but even more evidence distinguishes them from one another.

Identifying Those Jesus Raises from the Dead

Although already mentioned, it's important to emphasize the different groups Jesus raises from the dead in His two returns.

At the Rapture, the Lord will raise the "dead in Christ" (1 Thessalonians 4:16). This consists of those who are members of the Body of Christ because they have put their trust in the Savior since the Day of Pentecost. It's this large group of untold millions of New Testament saints to whom Jesus will give immortal bodies at the Rapture.

This is not, however, the same group John writes about in Revelation 20:4. These are the ones we refer to as "Tribulation saints," who make their appearance earlier in the book as those martyred because of their faith in Jesus during this time (Revelation 6:9–11, 7:9–17). It's this group that comes back to life after the Second Coming.

The resurrection of the dead at the time of Rapture includes *all* those who have died in Christ up to that moment. After Jesus returns to the earth following the Tribulation, He raises a *subset* of believers, those who "had been beheaded for the testimony of Jesus and for the word of God" (20:4). All the saints who perish during the Tribulation will receive their imperishable bodies after Jesus' return to the earth.

The identity of those Jesus brings back to life differentiates the two events.

Destination of the Saints

Just as the "comings and goings" of Scripture tell us Jesus receives the kingdom at His return to the earth rather than at His ascension, they also enable us to distinguish the Rapture from the Second Coming. As author and Bible prophecy scholar Dr. Ron Rhodes wrote:

> The pretribulation rapture involves Christ coming for His saints in the air before the tribulation, whereas at the second coming He will come back with His saints to the earth to reign for 1,000 years (Revelation 19; 20:1-6).[68]

At the Rapture, we go up to Heaven. Jesus made this clear when He introduced our expectation of His appearing in the Upper Room:

> In my Father's house are many rooms. If it were not so, would I have told you that I go to prepare a place for you? And if I go and

prepare a place for you, I will come again and will take you to myself, that where I am you may be also. (John 14:2–3)

In the above verses, He promises to take us to where He now resides; He doesn't say He is coming to be where we dwell. Isn't this a crucial distinction between the Rapture and Second Coming?

In my book, *The Triumph of the Redeemed,* I wrote:

The Greek word for "place" in John 14:2–3 denotes a physical residence. Jesus is preparing a *physical* room for us in His "Father's house." Why would He mention actual rooms within His "Father's house" in heaven in this context if He didn't intend to take us there? What's the purpose of mentioning the physical "place" He's preparing for us if it's not His intent to take us there when He comes for us?[69]

The words of Paul in Colossians 3:4 also emphasize that when Jesus comes for us, we go to Heaven: "When Christ who is your life appears, then you also will appear with him in glory."

Glory is not a place on earth. It doesn't describe our current world, nor does it fit anywhere here below before or at the end of the Tribulation period.

In the numerous references to the Second Coming throughout Scripture, the destination is always the earth. The writers never mention a return to Heaven, such as we see in many of the texts concerning the Rapture. In all the accounts of Jesus' return to the earth, the feet of those alive never leave the ground.

Zechariah 14:1–4 reveals that, at the end of the Tribulation, Jesus' feet will touch down on the Mount of Olives. After that, He sends out His angels to gather "the elect" to Himself (Matthew 24:31). Why would this be necessary if we've already met Him in the air and have come back to earth with Him?

Transformation of Living Saints

As noted in the previous chapter, a key aspect of Christ's appearing is the dramatic and instantaneous transformation of living believers. The

Apostle Paul emphasizes this in 1 Corinthians 15:47–54 and Philippians 3:20–21. In the following verses, He makes "the redemption of our bodies" a central feature of our hope:

> And not only the creation, but we ourselves, who have the first-fruits of the Spirit, groan inwardly as we wait eagerly for adoption as sons, the redemption of our bodies. For in this hope we were saved. Now hope that is seen is not hope. For who hopes for what he sees? But if we hope for what we do not see, we wait for it with patience. (Romans 8:23–25)

The New Testament teaches that the redemption of our bodies into those like that of our Risen Savior happens at the moment of the Rapture.

In all the biblical texts relating to the Second Coming, there's no mention of the Lord granting immortality to living saints. As we will see in the next section, the lack of such a change is an absolute necessity for what the Bible says will happen during the Millennium.

The Presence of Sin During the Millennium

Those who combine the Rapture and Second Coming can't reconcile this position with how the Bible describes life in Jesus' thousand-year reign, during which time people continue to sin and, at the end of that period, rebel against the Lord. If everyone receives an incorruptible body at the Second Coming, then such a scenario becomes impossible.

If everyone were to receive incorruptible bodies at Jesus' return to the earth, no one would refuse to participate in the Feast of Booths during Jesus' reign (Zechariah 14:16–19). No one would die during this time, as Isaiah states will happen (Isaiah 65:20). Who would rebel at the end of Jesus' reign if everyone entered His kingdom without the ability to sin (Revelation 20:7–10)?

At His appearing, Jesus will give all believers—whether alive or dead—glorified, gloriously transformed bodies (Philippians 3:20–21; 1 Corinthians 15:51–55). If we consider the Rapture and Second Coming occurring at the same time, no one would enter the millennial kingdom in natural bodies. That would make both sin and reproduction impossible during the thousand-year rule of Jesus.

We learn from both the Old and New Testaments that sin will exist when Jesus reigns over the nations. Psalm 2:8–9 tells He will rule with a "rod of iron," a fact that's repeated in Revelation 19:15 in reference to His Second Coming. If everyone enters the kingdom incapable of sinning, there's no need for such a rule.

American pastor and author John MacArthur sums up this critical distinction between the two events:

> If God raptures and glorifies all believers just prior to the inauguration of the millennial kingdom (as a posttribulational Rapture demands), no one would be left to populate and propagate the earthly kingdom of Christ promised to Israel. It is not within the Lord's plan and purpose to use glorified individuals to propagate the earth during the Millennium. Therefore, the Rapture needs to occur earlier so that after God has raptured all believers, He can save more souls—including Israel's remnant—during the seven-year Tribulation. Those people can then enter the millennial kingdom in earthly form.[70]

Since Scripture reveals that some believers will survive the Tribulation and enter the kingdom in natural bodies, there must be an interval between the Rapture and Second Coming so people have the opportunity to come to saving faith and somehow remain alive during the terrors of the Tribulation.

This by itself doesn't prove the pre-Tribulation appearing of Jesus, but it does require that a significant amount of time elapses before His return to the earth.

Other Key Differences

Below are three additional reasons explaining why it's impossible for the Rapture and Second Coming to be the same event. Even some who claim to hold a post-Tribulation view of the Rapture maintain that the Rapture happens before the bowl judgments of Revelation chapter 16, with the Church later returning with Jesus (Revelation 19:11–16). They recognize that the two can't be identical.

Other key differences include:

1. The Duration of the Two Events

When Jesus comes for His Church, it will happen quickly. First Corinthians 15:51 tells us it will happen "in a moment, in the twinkling of an eye." In Revelation 3:11, Jesus says that He's "coming quickly."

The Second Coming will consist of many events, with each one possibly taking several hours to several days. Observers will witness Jesus parading across the sky with us before He arrives in Israel to destroy the armies of the world gathered to stop Him from restoring a kingdom to Israel and inaugurating His millennial rule.

This difference confirms that the two events can't be the same. One happens almost instantaneously, while the other takes place over a much longer period.

2. The Mystery of the Rapture

In 1 Corinthians 15:51, Paul begins his discussion of the Lord's appearing with these words: "Behold! I tell you a mystery." The use of the word "mystery" in the New Testament differs from our ordinary understanding of it. My wife and I like to watch mystery movies, but that isn't the sense of the apostle's words in this context.

Instead, the word here designates new revelation, a truth God did not reveal in the Old Testament, but did later, through His apostles. When Paul introduces the Lord's return for His Church in the book of 1 Thessalonians, he says, "For this we declare to you by a word from the Lord" (4:15). This signified new revelation regarding the prominent place of the "dead in Christ" during the Rapture.

The Second Coming was certainly not something new during the New Testament era. Almost all the Old Testament prophetic books refer to it in some way, as do a substantial number of passages throughout the Psalms. Even Enoch wrote about it (Jude 14).

The concept of Jesus taking His Church away from the earth, however, was something entirely new.

3. The Differing Emphasis

The message of Rapture exudes both comfort and joyous expectation for believers. Paul emphasized this in 1 Thessalonians 4:18 and 5:11 as he encouraged His readers to "encourage one another" with his words regarding their eagerness to meet Jesus in the air.

The central feature of the Second Coming is judgment. When Jesus arrives on the scene, He destroys the armies gathered against Him, throws Antichrist and the False Prophet into the lake of fire, locks up Satan for a thousand years, and gathers those who survive the Tribulation before His throne for judgment (Revelation 19:19–20:4). The separation of the goats from the sheep, as recorded in Matthew 25:31–46, occurs after Jesus' return to the earth.

I'm sure many other differences exist; however, those given throughout this chapter suffice to clearly set the two events apart. There must be a meaningful gap in time between the Rapture and Jesus' return to the earth to allow people to come to saving faith and enter the Millennium with their natural bodies capable of reproducing as well as rebelling against the Lord.

How do we know the entire seven-year Tribulation happens in the interlude between the two? That's the topic of the upcoming chapters.

✑ Wisdom defends the pre-Tribulation Rapture by:

1. Confirming our unique place as the Body of Christ and heirs to His kingdom rather than current possessors of it.
2. Verifying that the Rapture, as described in 1 Thessalonians 4:13–17, must happen if the Bible is true.
3. Demonstrating that the Rapture and Second Coming are two distinct events separated by a significant period of time.

Chapter 18

INTERVENTION AND
DELIVERANCE

> One of the strongest arguments for a pretribulation rapture is the
> promise that the church will not see the wrath of God that is coming
> upon the world at the end of the age. This promise is clearly stated
> in 1 Thessalonians 1:10 and 5:9-10.[71]
>
> —Lee W. Brainard, *Ten Potent Proofs for the Pretribulation Rapture*

The Lord promised to deliver us from the future time of wrath the
Bible identifies as the Day of the Lord (1 Thessalonians 5:1–10).
He did so in the same context as he described the *harpazo*, our meeting
of Jesus in the air.

It's essential to keep in mind that John wrote the last book of the Bible
almost forty-five years after Paul wrote to the church at Thessalonica. If the
timing had been different, the apostle might have pointed us to the precise
place in the apocalypse where Jesus comes for His Church. We don't have
such a connection, but as we compare what Paul wrote with the book of
Revelation and the Old Testament teaching on the Day of the Lord, a clear
picture emerges that enables us to make just such a connection.

Most of those who deny our hope in Jesus' imminent appearing
exclude the Day of the Lord from their theology. It's as though the many
Scriptures that pertain to this time don't exist. They allegorize them along
with ones that promise the Lord's future restoration of Israel.

Why does this matter? Since, as we saw in chapter 9, the prophecies
concerning this day remain unfulfilled, we have a framework to better

understand 1 Thessalonians 5:1–10. This enables us to make a compelling case for placing Rapture *before* the Day of the Lord. And, given the strong correlation between it and the judgments recorded in Revelation, Jesus must come for us before this time of wrath on the earth begins.

With this in mind, I believe the following text provides the strongest proof for a pre-Tribulation Rapture. These verses affirm that we will miss the entire time of God's fierce judgment upon the planet:

> Now concerning the times and the seasons, brothers, you have no need to have anything written to you. For you yourselves are fully aware that the day of the Lord will come like a thief in the night. While people are saying, "There is peace and security," then sudden destruction will come upon them as labor pains come upon a pregnant woman, and they will not escape. But you are not in darkness, brothers, for that day to surprise you like a thief. For you are all children of light, children of the day. We are not of the night or of the darkness. So then let us not sleep, as others do, but let us keep awake and be sober. For those who sleep, sleep at night, and those who get drunk, are drunk at night. But since we belong to the day, let us be sober, having put on the breastplate of faith and love, and for a helmet the hope of salvation. For God has not destined us for wrath, but to obtain salvation through our Lord Jesus Christ, who died for us so that whether we are awake or asleep we might live with him. (1 Thessalonians 5:1–10)

In the above passage, the Lord guarantees that New Testament saints will not experience the outpouring of God's wrath during this coming day because He will come for us before it begins.

Why am I so sure? Let's begin by answering some critical questions regarding the above passage from 1 Thessalonians 5.

What Is the Wrath?

In 1 Thessalonians 1:10, Paul refers to Jesus as the one "who delivers us from the wrath to come." In 5:9, we have another assurance that "God has not destined us for wrath." What is the "wrath" from which the apostle promises our escape in these verses?

The context of 1 Thessalonians 5 points us back to the "sudden destruction" that will mark the start of the Day of the Lord (v. 3). The "wrath" in this context is the substance of all the judgments associated with this time of death and destruction that will come upon the world during the last days.

In his book defending the pre-Tribulation Rapture, author and Bible prophecy expert Lee W. Brainard presents three key reasons the apostle's mention of "wrath" in 1 Thessalonians 1:10 and 5:9 must refer to a future period of God's fury upon the earth:

First of all, when the Bible presents eternal wrath in the lake of fire, it does so with contextual clues such as mentions of fire, gehenna, outer darkness, eternal torment, eternal punishment, and wailing and gnashing of teeth. Such clues are lacking in the context of the two verses cited above....

Secondly, these promises of deliverance from the coming wrath can't be references to eternal wrath because Christians are already delivered from that awful reality. Our deliverance from eternal punishment is a historical fact, not a future event....

Thirdly, both of these verses involve a separation of mankind before the wrath is poured out on earth.... We go up, the wrath comes down.[72]

Another key reason to identify the wrath in such a way comes from the book of 2 Thessalonians, wherein Paul addresses the panic that erupted among these early saints (2:2–3). Someone claiming to represent his apostolic authority had told the Thessalonian saints that the Day of the Lord had already begun. This news terrified them.

If the wrath of this time applied to our eternal destiny of the unsaved, there's no reason this claim would cause so much fear. They already possessed eternal life. Wouldn't the fact that they were still alive seal the deal?

Why would they descend into a state of sheer panic because of the news of something that could only happen after this life?

They understood Paul's reference to the Day of Lord wrath as the devastation and death that would take place on the earth *after* their departure. They believed his promise that the Rapture would happen before the judgments of this day, which the apostle had told them about during his brief stay in Thessalonica.

Who Are "Them" and "We"?

As we continue our examination of 1 Thessalonians 5:1–11, it's important to note who the apostle says will be surprised by the "sudden destruction" at the start of the Day of the Lord and who will not. Clearly a separation takes place, with some experiencing the full impact of God's wrath while others will not.

The ones upon whom the "sudden destruction" will fall are those who are proclaiming, "There is peace and security." Paul adds that the "sudden destruction…will come upon them as labor pains come upon a pregnant woman," and says, "they will not escape" (5:3). The unbelievers of the world are referenced by the pronoun "them" in the text. They will remain unaware of the coming judgments until it's too late. They will fall for the lie that all is well and, as a result, will put their confidence in human wisdom rather than Jesus.

The extended period of wrath that defines the Day of the Lord will fall upon those outside of belief in Christ for salvation, those characterized by thinking the threats posed in this modern era will not spoil their aspirations for the future.

Paul then adds these initial words of encouragement for his readers:

But you are not in darkness, brothers, for that day to surprise you like a thief. For you are all children of light, children of the day. We are not of the night or of the darkness. (1 Thessalonians 5:4–5)

"We," in this context, refers to all those who have placed their faith in Christ who will *not* experience the perils of this coming time. As the apostle explains in verses 6–9, we, the "children of the day" are *not* "destined for the wrath" or "sudden destruction" that will mark the start of woes for the world, but "we will obtain salvation through our Lord Jesus Christ" (5:9–10).

Since the text is not about Hell, the "salvation" of which Paul writes isn't our response to the Gospel, but rather our future *deliverance* from it "through our Lord Jesus Christ." This is the Rapture, which the apostle described in 1 Thessalonians 4:13–17. The Greek word translated "salvation" in 5:9 has the primary meaning of "deliverance." Jesus will come for His Church before the wrath of the Day of the Lord falls upon the unsuspecting world.

There's unspeakably good news in these words. We will not experience the wrath of the Day of Lord, this extended time of God's fury described in the Old Testament and detailed in Revelation chapters 6–18.

Let's now recap what we know. It's clear that the Day of the Lord lies in the future and will include an extended time of widespread destruction and death. The Old Testament descriptions of it closely align with the seal, trumpet, and bowl judgments described in the book of Revelation.

As we follow the historical-grammatical method of biblical interpretation, which gives the words of Scripture their proper place, we're led to conclude that Revelation chapters 6–19 provide a futuristic account of how the Old Testament describes the Day of the Lord. The panic of the Thessalonian saints indicates they know a lot about these prophecies and understood Paul's words in 1 Thessalonians 5:9–10 as a promise of deliverance from them: "For God has not destined us for wrath, but to obtain salvation through our Lord Jesus Christ, who died for us so that whether we are awake or asleep we might live with him."

Doesn't this confirm a pre-Tribulation Rapture? Christ, through the Apostle Paul, promises that believers will experience deliverance before the start of the time that will greatly surprise those who aren't part of the Body of Christ.

The Lord will surely intervene in our world; He will make His presence known to all. His intervention signals our deliverance from the wrath that will fall on the earth after we leave.

What Is the Encouragement?

Paul concludes the passage concerning the Day of the Lord with these words: "Therefore encourage one another and build one another up, just as you are doing" (1 Thessalonians 5:11).

The only way this passage provides even the slightest bit of comfort must result from understanding that the Rapture will happen before the awful period begins. How would this be possible if the Lord intended for His Church to experience the series of judgments that will comprise the Day of the Lord?

This passage also assures us that Jesus will not leave any saint behind when He comes for us, not one. Let me explain.

In 1 Thessalonians 4:13–18, Paul distinguishes between living and dead saints. Because of this, many assume he has the same distinction in mind in 1 Thessalonians 5:10, where he mentions those "who died for us so that whether we are awake or asleep we might live with him."

However, the apostle has something else in mind in 5:10, as the words he uses for being "awake" and "asleep" differ from those he used in 1 Thessalonians 4:15–17. As such, they align much more closely with the preceding verses that differentiate between those who are spiritually awake versus those who are asleep in their walk with the Lord.

The Greek verb Paul uses for "awake" in verse 10 is *gregoreo*, which denotes moral alertness. In 5:4–8, Paul uses the word along with that of being "sober" to portray the idea of temperance in our walk with the Lord versus that of drunkenness or carelessness. "So then let us not sleep, as others do, but let us keep awake and be sober" (v. 6). Jesus used the word *gregoreo* in Matthew 24:42 and Mark 13:35 to indicate watchfulness for His return.

The word Paul uses for believers who are "asleep" in 5:10 is *katheudo*. This word most often refers to someone who is physically asleep, not dead. Of the twenty-two times this word appears in the New Testament, it only once refers to someone who had died. That instance is when Jesus used the word to refer to the girl He intended to raise from the dead. In 1 Thessalonians 4:17, Paul uses a different Greek word, *zao*, to refer to the saints who would be alive at the time of the Rapture.

In 1 Thessalonians 5:4–8, the apostle uses *katheudo* to designate believers who are asleep in their walk with the Lord (v. 6) and contrasts them with sober saints, or those who are *gregoreo*.

Based on Paul's usage of the same words in the preceding context, as well as in 1 Thessalonians 5:10, we know His reference to believers who are "awake" and "asleep" is much different than 1 Thessalonians 4:13–17. It leads us to this wonderful assurance: When the Lord comes for His Church, He will take all those who are alert spiritually as well as all those who are asleep in their walk with Him. He will not leave one saint behind. If you are "in Christ," you meet Jesus in the air.

Because of what the New Testament tells us about the judgment seat of Christ and our rewards, we understand the advantages of living in a way that reflects spiritual alertness rather than neglects one's faith. Even so, Jesus will not leave any born-again saint behind when He comes for us. To claim otherwise contradicts what the Bible reveals about God's great grace and mercy.

Being "in Christ" guarantees our heavenward journey when He appears.

⸎ *Wisdom defends the pre-Tribulation Rapture by:*

1. **Confirming our unique place as the Body of Christ and heirs to His kingdom rather than current possessors of it.**
2. **Verifying that the Rapture, as described in 1 Thessalonians 4:13–17, must happen if the Bible is true.**
3. **Demonstrating that the Rapture and Second Coming are two distinct events separated by a significant period of time.**
4. **Promising to keep the Body of Christ out of the Day of the Lord wrath that will suddenly fall upon the unbelieving world in the last days.**

Chapter 19

THE BELIEVING
WILL BE LEAVING

What Paul is saying to the beleaguered and bewildered Thessalonians who were deceived by forged letters allegedly having emanated from Paul indicating that the Day of the Lord had already begun, is that they could not possibly be in the tribulation period because they are still physically present on planet earth....the tribulation period itself will not take place until there is first a physical removal of the church via the rapture.[73]

Andy Woods, *The Falling Away*

After Paul wrote his first letter to the Thessalonians, someone sent a message to the believers in that city claiming that the Day of the Lord had already begun. Because this errant news plunged the church there into a state of panic, Paul quickly wrote them a second letter, in which he addressed this matter:

Now concerning the coming of our Lord Jesus Christ and our being gathered together to him, we ask you, brothers, not to be quickly shaken in mind or alarmed, either by a spirit or a spoken word, or a letter seeming to be from us to the effect that the day of the Lord has come. Let no one deceive you in any way. For that day will not come, unless the rebellion comes first, and the man of lawlessness is revealed, the son of destruction. (2 Thessalonians 2:1–3)

Paul began his response by reminding his readers about their ultimate hope in Jesus' return for them (v. 1). The Rapture is when all the saints will be "gathered together to" the Lord, just as the apostle wrote in 1 Thessalonians 4:13–17. This would also remind the Thessalonians of the Lord's comforting promise of deliverance from the wrath of the Day of the Lord at His appearing (1 Thessalonians 5:9–10).

The apostle addressed their fears by telling them "not to be quickly shaken in mind or alarmed." Bible scholar and commentator D. Edmond Hiebert wrote the following about these words: "The verb *shaken* denotes a rocking motion, a shaking up and down, like a building shaken by an earthquake."[74] He added that to be "alarmed" signifies a feeling of "fright," with its usage here conveying a "state of alarm, of nervous excitement."[75] The news regarding the start of the Day of the Lord caused the Thessalonian believers to physically tremble with fear.

Their frayed nerves confirm a couple of things. First, Paul's description of what happens during the Day of the Lord came from the Old Testament passages regarding the death and destruction of this period, which accounts for the Thessalonians' panic upon hearing that this time had begun. Second, it indicates they believed the Rapture would happen first. Why else would they have responded with such great anxiety at the thought that it had begun while they remained earthbound?

In verse 3, Paul explains how they, as well as believers today by application, can know for sure that this time of terror hasn't yet started. Two specific events would mark its beginning:

1. "The rebellion" or "the apostasy" in other translations.
2. The revealing of the "man of lawlessness," or Antichrist.

Until the past few years, I considered the first indicator as a falling away of the Church from the truth of God's Word, or what normally comes to mind when we think of "apostasy." For reasons I'll discuss later in this chapter, I've come to believe this refers to the Rapture. The Greek word *apostasia* can denote a physical departure.

Author and Bible prophecy expert Dr. Ron Rhodes wrote the following about this alternative interpretation of 2 Thessalonians 2:3:

Bible Scholars E. Schuyler English, Andy Woods, and Wayne House, among many others, have raised the possibility that yet another translation may be preferable here: "Let no one deceive you in any way. For that will not come, unless the departure comes first, and the man of lawlessness is revealed, the son of destruction." If this translation is correct, then the statement that "the departure comes first" is compelling evidence of pretribulationism.

The evidence for this view is substantial.[76]

I realize that it's controversial to regard *apostasia* as a physical departure and hence a reference to the pre-Tribulation Rapture. Many highly respected proponents of the pre-Tribulation Rapture disagree with me on this. Because I respect their differing take regarding this matter, I considered skipping this topic, but decided to include it because of how such a discussion verifies our mutual belief regarding the placement of Jesus' appearance before the Tribulation.

The Rapture Delivers Us from the Day of the Lord

The first reason for regarding the *apostasia* as the Rapture comes from 1 Thessalonians 5:1–10, in which the Lord promises to deliver us from the wrath of the Day of the Lord via the Rapture. Doesn't it make sense that the apostle would first calm their anxiety by reminding them of their hope of meeting Jesus in the air? What better way to assure them the time of wrath had not yet arrived than by reminding them of their guaranteed deliverance from it?

I believe the Day of the Lord starts with the Rapture of the Church, followed at some point by Antichrist's covenant with Israel and "the many," which begins what we regard as the seven-year Tribulation. Jesus appearing to take His Church out of the world will mark the start of His dramatic intervention in the affairs of humanity, which is what this coming period is all about.

Author and former professor at Dallas Theological Seminary, J. Dwight Pentecost, wrote the following in his magnificent work, *Things to Come,* where he also equates the Rapture with the surprise start to the future time of wrath upon the earth:

> If the Day of the Lord did not begin until the second advent, since that event is preceded by signs, the Day of the Lord could not come as a "thief in the night," unexpected, and unheralded, as it is said it will come in 1 Thessalonians 5:2. The only way this day could break unexpectedly upon the world is to have it begin immediately after the rapture of the church.[77]

How does this support the translation of *apostasia* as a departure? If the Thessalonian saints understood that the Day of the Lord began with their removal from the earth, and I believe they did, then the fact that they remained earthbound would greatly comfort them. The fact that the Rapture "comes first," or before this terrible time of chaos and death on the earth, would confirm that this period had not yet started.

Equating the departure of 2 Thessalonians 2:3 to our removal from the planet also reassures us. We live during a time of great spiritual apostasy in the church. Many churches that once strictly adhered to the inerrancy and teachings of Scripture have drifted away to the point of adopting the world's standards for such issues as homosexuality, gay marriage, transgenderism, and, in many cases, the advocacy of abortion.

If *apostasia* refers to the church's departure from the faith, what assurance does that give us today that the time of God's wrath has not yet begun? For the past several decades, we've seen a great departure from the faith throughout many denominations.

Of course, we know this time hasn't yet begun because the "man of lawlessness" hasn't yet emerged on the world stage. Paul combines both of these indicators as definitive signs that the Day of the Lord had not yet arrived. The combination reveals the same conclusion to us.

Paul Refers to a Definite Event

I regard the strongest argument for regarding *apostasia* as a physical departure is Paul's referral to it as "**the** apostasy" (2 Thessalonians 2:3, emphasis added). The definite article indicates the apostle has a specific event in mind that his readers would *readily recognize* apart from any further clarification.[78]

If *apostasia* refers to a spiritual falling away, we might expect to find mention of it in the books Paul wrote to the Thessalonians, but such is not the case. The only "departure" his readers would be aware of is the Rapture, which he reminded them about in verse 1. He didn't write about the Church's departure from the faith until much later in his ministry,

If the apostle were referring to something other than Jesus' appearing, he would have provided an explanation to clarify his meaning for his readers, but that isn't what we see. He assumes the Thessalonian saints would readily understand what he meant by "the departure" or *apostasia*.

If such a falling away from the faith is to be a definitive sign that the Day of Lord hasn't yet begun, how can we distinguish it from the many other seasons of apostasy in the Church? In *The Triumph of the Redeemed*, I wrote:

> If *apostasia* refers to a spiritual falling away from the faith, how do we distinguish it from many such times in the history of the church when it has abandoned biblical teachings? Most of the organized church today has already departed *far, far away* from the beliefs handed down from the Lord to His apostles.[79]

During the Dark Ages, the Catholic Church departed far away from the purity of Gospel. During the twentieth century, modern-day liberalism invaded Christendom to the extent that many pastors denied the miracles as indicating the divinity of Jesus. Even today, many pastors of mainline denominations reject the physical resurrection of the Savior.

There have been multiple falling-aways from the faith during the history of the church, yet in 2 Thessalonians 2:3, Paul refers to a specific and identifiable event that would indicate the Day of the Lord has not yet arrived. The Rapture fits much better in this context than that of a defection from the faith.

Yes, the apostle later wrote about a spiritual forsaking of the faith, but his references fit within the time of the Church Age, not as a sign of the arrival of the Day of the Lord. When he wrote about people departing "from the faith" in 1 Timothy 4:1, he depicted it as a *pattern of behavior* that would characterize the Church in the "latter times." The same is true in 2 Timothy 4:3–5.

In 2 Thessalonians 2:3, the *apostasia* is a definitive and identifiable event. When the apostle later wrote about the falling away from the faith that would happen in the church, it was always in the context of observable patterns that the faithful could identify.

The Context

The only place Paul uses the word *apostasia* is in 2 Thessalonians 2:3. In 1 Timothy 4:1, he uses its verb form, *aphistemi*. In most of the New Testament instances, the verb refers to a physical departure, but here it refers to a spiritual defection from biblical truth that would characterize the "latter days." If the verb form of *apostasia* can refer to both a spiritual and a physical departure in Scripture, it seems reasonable to conclude that noun can refer to the latter. The leads to another determining factor in deciding between the two possible meanings: the context.

In his book, *The Falling Away*, Dr. Andy Woods provides considerable evidence in favor of regarding the "rebellion" as a physical departure based upon the context. He writes that the Greek word "*apostasia* simply means to 'to stand away from' or 'to depart.' Only by examining how it is used in its immediate context will determine what the departure is from, whether it be a spiritual or physical departure."[80]

He also explains that it's the surrounding verses, and even the writings of the author, that determine the context indicating whether *apostasia* refers to a physical departure or a spiritual falling away. It's the *context* that confirms our interpretation of the word.

Both the immediate context of 2 Thessalonians 2:3 and the purpose of the epistle point to a physical separation rather than one from the faith.

Second Thessalonians 2 begins with, "Now concerning the coming of our Lord Jesus Christ and our being gathered together to him" (v. 1), which would have reminded the readers of what Paul wrote concerning the Rapture in 1 Thessalonians 4:13–18. The immediate context points to the Rapture. Why would the apostle change the topic to a spiritual falling away without an additional a word of explanation?

Both Paul's letters to the Thessalonians favor the sense of *apostasia* as our physical removal from the earth. He refers to the Rapture throughout both epistles, mentioning it in almost every chapter. This event would've been foremost in the Thessalonian believers' minds as they read the second epistle.

Furthermore, there's no reference to spiritual apostasy in either of the letters, nor does it come up as a topic in other books until much later in Paul's ministry. And when it does, it surfaces as a general condition of the Church in the latter days rather than something identifiable such as would indicate the start of the Day of the Lord.

A little later in the context of 2 Thessalonians 2, Paul explains why the "man of lawlessness" can't make himself known until *after* the Day of the Lord begins:

And you know what is restraining him now so that he may be revealed in his time. For the mystery of lawlessness is already at work. Only he who now restrains it will do so until he is out of the way. (vv. 6–7)

If we identify the "restraining" force as the Holy Spirit's presence in the Body of Christ, and it's by far the most favored and likely interpretation, this becomes another argument for regarding *apostasia* as the Rapture. I say this because of the parallels with the identifying factors of the start of the Day of the Lord.

In verse 3, the *apostasia* happens "first" followed by the unveiling of the "man of lawlessness." In verses 6–7, we have the removal of the Holy Spirit's influence through New Testament believers, which allows the revelation of Antichrist's identity. In both cases, one follows the other.

If it's true that verses 6–7 tell us the Rapture permits the appearing of Antichrist on the world scene, and it is, doesn't it seem likely that this is also the intent behind verse 3? In both references, the Lord removes

His Church from the earth, which leads to the appearance of Satan's man.

An Example from Church History

Another factor that influences our interpretation of *apostasia* comes from a reference to the Rapture from early Church history. Cyprian (AD 200–258), the earlier-mentioned bishop in the city of Carthage during the third century AD, wrote the following:

> We who see that terrible things have begun, and know that still more terrible things are imminent, may regard it as the greatest advantage to depart from it as quickly as possible. Do you not give God thanks, do you not congratulate yourself, that by an early departure you are taken away, and delivered from the shipwrecks and disasters that are imminent?[81]

It's more than a little significant that Cyprian used the words "depart" and "early departure" to refer to the Lord appearing to take His Church away before a time of "shipwrecks and disasters." Although this alone wouldn't confirm translating *apostasia* as "departure," it lends considerable support. It's an instance of a noted Church father referring to the event we today call the Rapture as a "departure."

Conclusion

If *apostasia* in 2 Thessalonians 2:3 refers to our physical departure via the Rapture, and I believe it does, this provides rock-solid proof for placing it before the beginning of the seven-year Tribulation. There are several other arguments that others make in support of interpreting 2 Thessalonians 2:3 as a reference to the pre-Tribulation Rapture. I have recounted the ones I regard as the most persuasive.

Regardless of how one interprets *apostasia*, the New Testament confirms that we will depart the earth at Jesus' appearing.

℮⅗ Wisdom defends the pre-Tribulation Rapture by:

1. Confirming our unique place as the Body of Christ and heirs to His kingdom rather than current possessors of it.

2. Verifying that the Rapture, as described in 1 Thessalonians 4:13–17, must happen if the Bible is true.

3. Demonstrating that the Rapture and Second Coming are two distinct events separated by a significant period of time.

4. Promising to keep the Body of Christ out of the Day of the Lord wrath that will suddenly fall upon the unbelieving world in the last days.

5. Providing compelling proof that we will depart from the world before the start of the Day of the Lord.

Chapter 20

DESTINATION: HEAVEN

The idea of going to the Father's house in heaven was quite foreign to the thinking of the disciples. Their hope was that Christ would immediately establish His kingdom on earth and they would remain in the earthly sphere to reign with Him.... In making the pronouncement in John 14, Christ held before His disciples an entirely different hope than that which was promised to Israel.... The hope of the church is to be taken to heaven; the hope of Israel is Christ returning to reign over the earth.[82]

—John F. Walvoord, *The Rapture Question*

Some people are spontaneous; they leave home for vacation without a destination in mind. Some take long drives not knowing where the road might take them. I'm not like that; I like to have a clear end point in mind when I take a trip, whether long or short. Whenever I head out for several days, I line up hotel reservations well in advance.

Likewise, there's no uncertainty regarding our destination when Jesus appears; the Bible says He will take us to His "Father's house" (John 14:2). In the Upper Room on the night before His crucifixion, Jesus told His disciples about the Rapture in order to comfort them. Yes, He was going away, but He promised to return and take them to Heaven.

The words of the Apostle Paul have laid a firm foundation for our understanding of Jesus' appearing and provided much evidence for placing it before the coming time of God's wrath upon the earth, which seems especially near as I write. The Lord didn't say a whole lot about His return for the Church, but His words assure us of its imminence and destination.

Jesus Is Preparing a Place for Us in Heaven

Jesus' grand promise to His disciples continues to comfort us today with the message that He's preparing a special place for us in His "Father's house":

> In my Father's house are many rooms. If it were not so, would I have told you that I go to prepare a place for you? And if I go and prepare a place for you, I will come again and will take you to myself, that where I am you may be also. (John 14:2–3)

If one key factor distinguishes the Lord's promise in the above verses from the Second Coming, it's Jesus' words that He's coming so "that where I am you may be also." When the Rapture occurs, Jesus will take us to the place He is currently preparing for us.

Our Savior isn't going to meet us in the air to bring us back to earth. When He comes for us, Heaven will be our destination. Christ reserved our room in glory long ago, and He's now making sure our abode is ready for arrival.

Lee W. Brainard provides the following insight in his book, *Ten Potent Proofs of the Pretribulation Rapture*:

> Where did Jesus go when he left Earth? Heaven! Where is he now? In heaven! Where is the place that he is preparing for us? In heaven! Where will we be going when the Lord comes again for his church? Heaven! This should thrill us. When Jesus comes for us, he will take us to the heavenly city, where we will fine eternal residence in the Father's house in quarters custom-built for us by the Master Carpenter himself.[83]

Why would Jesus mention His "Father's house" in this context if it wasn't His intention to take us there? His words tell us that at the time of Rapture, He will take His followers—that's us—to His current residence in Heaven. As He explained a little bit later that same evening, one of His purposes in doing so is to show us His eternal splendor: "Father, I will that they also, whom thou hast given me, be with me where I am; that they may behold my glory, which thou hast given me: for thou loved me before the foundation of the world" (John 17:24).

Jesus uses the same expression in the above verse as in John 14:3, "where I am." In His prayer, He explains that He longs to bring us up to His Father's house so He might show us the full display of His glory.

In the John 14 text, Jesus also emphasizes that He's preparing "a place," or *topos*, for us. In nearly all of its ninety-plus usages in the New Testament, *topos* denotes a physical location. It frequently refers to a specific location such as a city, village, or area.

Please know that "Jesus is preparing *actual* rooms in His Father's house for the multitudes of people who will have come to know Him as their Savior since that evening. Our new home will feature many amenities that will nicely accommodate our immortal, resurrected bodies."[84]

The word Jesus chose for "prepare," *hetoimazo*, further designates our future home as both physical and tangible. Paul used this word when he asked Philemon to "prepare a lodging place" for him (Philemon 22). In Hebrews 11:16, the writer uses it in reference to the preparation of "a city," a reference to the New Jerusalem described in the last chapters of Revelation.

Can you see how the picture of Jesus constructing a place for us aligns with Wisdom's extravagant invitation recorded Proverbs 9:1–6? In both instances, there's preparation and extravagance. Based upon the words of Revelation 19:6–8, a wedding feast awaits us after Jesus takes us home to Heaven. If the "marriage supper of the Lamb" is anything like the Jewish celebrations of the first century AD, it will last as long as a week.

Please don't settle for the meager bread and water offered by those who suggest that our anticipation of a grand banquet in Heaven is somehow carnal and unspiritual. The Savior is making all the arrangements for it; how dare anyone regard His lavish provisions in such a way?

He Will Keep Us "From the Hour of Trial"

As a young pastor (now decades ago), I didn't regard Revelation 3:10–11a as particularly supportive of my pre-Tribulation Rapture position. I was mistaken. The more I examine this passage, the more I recognize these verses as the Lord's solemn vow to keep His Church out of all the judgments described in Revelation chapters 6–18.

> Because you have kept my word about patient endurance, I will keep you from the hour of trial that is coming on the whole world, to try those who dwell on the earth. I am coming soon. (Revelation 3:10–11a)

Jesus' words in these verses don't specify where He's taking us, but it's clear that we will leave the earth. This is the same event He spoke about to His disciples in the Upper Room. The elements of this promise clearly point to the pre-Tribulation Rapture.

What did Jesus mean by "the hour of trial that is coming on the whole world?" This isn't another persecution of the Church, because He tells us it will impact everyone on the planet regardless of what they believe. The earth has only experienced one such period when God's judgment affected everyone alive at the time: the Noahic Flood recorded in Genesis 6.

When might this "hour of trial" take place? The future judgments described in Revelation chapters 6–18 fit well with this description. They will strike all the people in the world with a severity that certainly qualifies as a "trial." As Paul did in 1 Thessalonians 5:1–10, the Lord provides us the identity of those who will absorb the brunt of the time and those who will miss it.

The Lord identifies those who experience the "hour of trial" as "those who dwell on the earth." John uses this phrase eight other times in the book of Revelation (6:10; 8:13; 11:10; 13:8–12, 14; 14:6; and 17:8). In each instance, "those who dwell on the earth" either refers either to people impacted by the Tribulation or to those refusing to repent of their sins during that time.

Lee Brainard describes "earth-dwellers" as a reference "to those humans whose hearts and lives are wrapped up in Earth and its concerns, in contrast to those who are pilgrims and strangers in it."[85]

The Lord's comforting pledge to those who belong to His true Church is that He "will keep us from" this grim time that will affect all peoples.

This isn't a promise to keep us safe *during* this time, rather, it's a vow to take us out of the earth *before* it begins.

> The verse plainly states that the Lord will *keep* his church *from* the hour of trial. Note the words KEEP FROM. This phrase does not mean *keep from harm* while in the hour or *preserve* while in the hour or *protect* while in the hour. It means *keep from the hour*, which implies removal prior to the hour.[86]

Does this signify a pre-Tribulation Rapture of the Church? Absolutely! Those who place the Rapture in the middle or at the end of the Tribulation say Jesus will keep believers safe throughout it, just as God protected the Israelites during the time of plagues in Egypt. Such an interpretation fails to take into account the key difference between what happened in Egypt long ago and what lies ahead for the world. Back then, God's people were isolated in the land of Goshen; they weren't spread out across the nation. No such clear distinction exists now, as believers and those who reject the Gospel live in the same communities. John F. Walvoord explained the difference this way:

> The character of the judgments that will fall is such that they will affect everyone—famine, pestilence, sword, earthquake, and stars falling from heaven. The only way one could be kept safe from that day of wrath would be to be delivered beforehand.[87]

If the Tribulation represents the wrath the world will experience during the Day of the Lord, we know that very few humans will remain alive at its conclusion. Jesus Himself said human life on the planet would end apart from His return cutting short this time (Matthew 24:22). If the Church experiences half of this coming day, most of its members will perish by the midpoint. By its end, very few would remain alive.

Author and Bible prophecy scholar Arnold Fruchtenbaum makes this same point in explaining why the promise of Revelation 3:10 can't possibly signify our protection *during* the Tribulation period:

Throughout the Tribulation, saints are being killed on a massive scale (Rev. 6:9-11; 11:7; 12:11; 13:7, 15; 17:6; 18:24). If these saints are *Church saints*, they are not being kept safe and Revelation 3:10 is meaningless. Only if *Church saints* and *Tribulation saints* are kept distinct does the promise of Revelation 3:10 make any sense.[88]

As we watch the Tribulation period rapidly approaching our world, we have Jesus' firm assurance that He will remove His Church before it arrives. This isn't wishful thinking or a desire to avoid torture and certain death. (Who would want to endure that, anyway?) It's firmly based on the Savior's words in Revelation 3:10. However, there's still more to His pledge regarding our safety.

"I Am Coming Quickly"

How does Jesus rescue us from this coming time? His gives us the answer in Revelation 3:11a: "I am coming soon." The connection between the Lord keeping His own people out of the Tribulation and His return for us is unmistakable. He will deliver us by taking us out of the world.

The Greek word for "soon" most accurately denotes an event that takes place "quickly."[89] Before this "hour of trial" begins, Jesus will come "quickly" to rescue us by taking us out of this world. As we noted in chapter 17, the Second Coming is by no means a quick event. The return Jesus has in mind here is the Rapture, which Paul says will happen in the "twinkling of an eye" (1 Corinthians 15:52).

Jesus' words from Revelation 3:11a are repeated two more times in the last chapter of the Bible. In fact, His last recorded words to His Church are, "I am coming quickly" (Revelation 22:20). Isn't it significant that the Lord's last words to us as a body of believers include His promise to take us away before His judgments sweep over the entire earth?

If His words, "I am coming quickly," in Revelation 3:11a must refer to the Rapture, isn't it reasonable to assume they carry the same intent in the last chapter of the book as well? In both instances, Jesus is addressing His Church, not the "earth-dwellers" who will endure the time of severe testing.

Jesus, who surely knows the end of human history as well as its beginning, said in Revelation 22:16: "I, Jesus, have sent my angel to testify to you about these things for the churches. I am the root and the descendant of David, the bright morning star."

Why would the Lord include such a strong statement concerning the events outlined in the book of Revelation? He knew the book, with its promises of His appearing, judgments upon the planet, and glorious Second Coming, would come under fierce attack throughout Church history. Today, as the time nears, even those who claim to adhere to the inspiration and inerrancy of Scripture scoff at our literal understanding of the events ahead for the world.

As if to put an exclamation point on our anticipation of arriving in Heaven with immortal bodies like that of our Savior, Revelation ends with these words: "He who testifies to these things says, 'Surely I am coming quickly.' Amen. Come, Lord Jesus!" (22:20).

ᴄ⸎ *Wisdom defends the pre-Tribulation Rapture by:*

1. Confirming our unique place as the Body of Christ and heirs to His kingdom rather than current possessors of it.
2. Verifying that the Rapture, as described in 1 Thessalonians 4:13–17, must happen if the Bible is true.
3. Demonstrating that the Rapture and Second Coming are two distinct events separated by a significant period of time.
4. Promising to keep the Body of Christ out of the Day of the Lord wrath that will suddenly fall upon the unbelieving world in the last days.
5. Providing compelling proof that we will depart from the world before the start of the Day of the Lord.
6. Assuring us that Heaven will be our destination when Jesus appears to take us home.

Chapter 21

WE'RE ALREADY THERE

What is said of the twenty-four elders could not be true of angelic beings, for angels are not crowned with victors' crowns (*stephanos*) received as rewards, nor are they seated on thrones (*thronas*), which throne speaks of royal dignity and prerogative, nor are angels robbed in white as a result of judgment. The impossibility of this view argues for the second view which sees them as resurrected redeemed men, who are clothed, crowned, and seated on thrones in connection with royalty in heaven.[90]

–J. Dwight Pentecost, *Things to Come*

I have no memories of my high school graduation party, but I vividly remember the ceremony that preceded it. An announcement over the loudspeaker suddenly interrupted the playing of Edward Elgar's "Pomp and Circumstance" with the news that a thunderstorm was approaching the outdoor stadium. The man asked everyone to make their way indoors to the nearby gymnasium, which had been set up for the ceremony in case of rain.

Since I was also playing in the orchestra that day, I picked up my music stand and trombone and walked with the throngs of people leaving the stands. A downpour drenched many of us before we reached the gym's doors.

I know a celebration soon followed at my home, because I have pictures of it. In one, I'm standing behind a cake inscribed with appropriate congratulations.

But what does this have to do Bible prophecy? It's not photos of the past that place us in Heaven before the start of the Tribulation, but what the Lord showed John after He brought him there. As the apostle witnessed the scene around God's throne leading up to the Lamb opening the seals to the scroll, he reveals the presence of twenty-four elders (Revelation 4:1–5:16). If this group represents the Church, it means we are already with the Lord in Paradise before the beginning of the sequence of judgments described in Revelation chapters 6–18.

If these elders represent the Church, then just as pictures from the past verify my family's celebration of my high school graduation, so John's vision of the future tells us we are already with the Lord before the Tribulation woes begin.

With this in mind, let's look at the evidence backing up the claim that this group of twenty-four represents New Testament saints who have already received their resurrection bodies and stood before Christ at the bema seat (where believers stand before Christ to receive rewards based upon their actions for Him on earth).

They Aren't Angelic Beings

Because the sights and sounds of Revelations chapters 4–5 happen in God's presence with the Lamb, Jesus, later taking center stage, one might first assume the twenty-four elders represent a class of heavenly beings. As we examine what they say about themselves, along with John's description of them, it becomes apparent that such an identification is not possible.

Arnold Fruchtenbaum, in his masterful work, *The Footsteps of the Messiah*, lists several clues from the text that negate recognizing the elders as angels.[91] I will start with his thoughts and expand upon them.

Fruchtenbaum begins by pointing out the "elders are clothed with white garments, which throughout Revelation are symbols of salvation."[92] This picture of Christ's imputed righteousness for New Testament saints doesn't fit with the angels who didn't rebel against God and thus never needed redemption. The white robes speak to those who are blameless solely because of Jesus and His death on the cross, which the elders themselves confirm in Revelation 5:9 as they identify themselves as "ransomed people for God." These words don't apply to angels.

There's also the matter of the "golden crowns" on the heads of the elders, which they throw before the throne of God (Revelation 4:4, 10). Fruchtenbaum explains why this reference alone excludes depicting the group of twenty-four as angels.

> These crowns are not diadems worn by those who are royal by nature, which would have been the case had they been celestial beings. They crowns are *stephanos* crowns, the crowns of over-comers given as rewards to the members of the church at the judgment seat of Messiah.[93]

Additionally, John pictures the elders as sitting on thrones (Revelation 4:4), denoting rule and authority. The Bible never depicts angels in this way; it reserves the privilege of ruling with Christ exclusively for New Testament and Tribulation saints. This promise is exclusively for those redeemed by Jesus' blood since the Day of Pentecost.

Another clue that excludes identifying the members of the group as angels comes from the word the apostle uses describe the twenty-four: "elders." In Scripture, this term always applies to men and never to angels. It also connotes an aging process, which also eliminates angels.

In Scripture, the word "elders" only refers to those in authority among God's people, whether in Israel or the Church. We see various levels of authority among the angelic beings (Ephesians 6:12); however, this term isn't found in Scripture in reference to their leadership structure.

Why have I put so much effort into refuting the possibility that angels are the twenty-four elders? Because it's easy to assume such an identification with just a casual reading of the text, and as we narrow our quest to classify them as representatives of the Church, we find further proof that verifies our belief in the pre-Tribulation Rapture.

Can The Elders Be Other Saints?

If not angels, are there other groups of biblical saints the twenty-four elders might represent? Evidence from the text confines our answer to resurrected believers who have already received their immortal bodies and, as we saw tin the previous section, already appeared before the judgment seat of Christ.

The elders' "white garments" (Revelation 4:4) are identical to the dress of believers as seen at marriage feast of the Lamb (19:6–8). Since they already adorn the clothing depicted in the scenes of Revelation 19, including when they return to earth with Jesus (verse 16), it confirms that this group has already experienced the Rapture as described in 1 Corinthians 15:51–55.

Author and commentator John MacArthur wrote:

> Christ promised the believers at Sardis that they would "be clothed in white garments" (3:5) .... White garments symbolize Christ's righteousness imputed to believers at salvation.[94]

The elders can't be Tribulation saints in Heaven, because the picture of them standing before God's throne happens after Jesus opens several of the seals (Revelation 6:9–11), and John later identifies them as a group separate from the elders (7:13). Furthermore, Jesus doesn't raise them from the dead until after His return to the earth (Revelation 20:1–4). Yes, they will also reign with Jesus in His millennial kingdom, but they will receive their immortal bodies after the Second Coming.

Although both Old Testament and Tribulation saints have a presence with the Lord in Heaven before their bodily resurrection at Jesus' return to the earth, the above factors depict the elders John describes in Revelation chapters 4–5 as representing the Church. The crowns, white robes, and thrones point to resurrected saints who have already appeared before the bema seat of Christ, received their rewards, and been assigned positions of authority in the coming kingdom.

Why Is This Significant?

If the twenty-four elders represent the redeemed whom Christ has already resurrected from the dead and gloriously transformed at His appearing (1 Corinthians 15:47–55), as the evidence suggests, it provides additional proof of the pre-Tribulation Rapture.

Author Lee Brainard sums up the significance of identifying this group as the Church:

> The twenty-four elders, once identified, provide us perhaps the most potent argument for a pretribulation rapture in the Bible. They can't be angels because they are redeemed by the blood of the Lamb. They can't be Old Testament saints waiting for their resurrection at the second coming because they already have their rewards. They can't be New Testament saints waiting for resurrection because they already have their rewards. They can only be New Testament saints who have already enjoyed the resurrection.[95]

If we as resurrected and glorified saints witness the Lamb's opening of the seals in Heaven, how is it possible that we can also be on earth to experience these judgments? Isn't it encouraging to know we'll be with Jesus in Heaven before the Lamb releases the riders of the Apocalypse to wreak havoc, suffering, destruction, and death upon the earth?

We live at a time when the events John describes in Revelation chapter 6 seem to be so close that many believe they've already begun. I'm convinced the Lord's restraining hand over the affairs of this world alone accounts for the fact that the riders of the apocalypse (Revelation 6:1–8) haven't yet made their appearance on the earth. The Holy Spirit is even now keeping the "man of lawlessness" from making himself known (2 Thessalonians 2:3–8).

Jesus' imminent appearing calms my heart as nothing else can when I look at the world around me; it encourages me to keep serving Him. He will intervene in our world in the near future, and after that, nothing will be normal as Satan hastens to put his agenda of death and destruction into full gear in his futile attempt to stop Jesus' inheritance of the nations.

Is it any wonder the biblically sound teaching of the pre-Tribulation Rapture is one of the most attacked doctrines today? Our enemy knows that, as believers, we need the consolation it offers as we watch darkness overshadow our world. The devil understands biblical prophecy and knows the Lord is right at the door, ready to rescue us before the time of testing overwhelms the entire planet.

The Lord intended the doctrine of the pre-Tribulation to be a rich source of mutual encouragement (1 Thessalonians 4:18, 5:11); and it's surely all that and much more.

ᜐ Wisdom defends the pre-Tribulation Rapture by:

1. Confirming our unique place as the Body of Christ and heirs to His kingdom rather than current possessors of it.
2. Verifying that the Rapture, as described in 1 Thessalonians 4:13–17, must happen if the Bible is true.
3. Demonstrating that the Rapture and Second Coming are two distinct events separated by a significant period of time.
4. Promising to keep the Body of Christ out of the Day of the Lord wrath that will suddenly fall upon the unbelieving world in the last days.
5. Providing compelling proof that we will depart from the world before the start of the Day of the Lord.
6. Assuring us that Heaven will be our destination when Jesus appears to take us home.
7. Picturing resurrected New Testament saints in Heaven, with the Lamb, before He opens the seals that initiate the Tribulation judgments. We're already there before the Tribulation starts.

Chapter 22

WHAT ABOUT
THE GREAT COMMISSION?

In the last days, God will have the gospel message proclaimed worldwide so that people are without excuse about making a decision for
Christ. During the first half of the tribulation, God not only uses
the 144,000 Israelites from each of the twelve tribes who reach "a
great multitude which no one could number" (Revelation 7:9), but
he also establishes in and around Jerusalem two special witnesses
endowed with supernatural powers.[96]

Ed Hindson, *Future Glory*

Most pastors preach at least one sermon a year on Matthew
28:19–20 emphasizing Jesus' command to "make disciples of all
nations." Along with that, they emphasize the words of Acts 1:8, where
we read that Jesus instructed His followers to be His "witnesses": "But
you will receive power when the Holy Spirit has come upon you, and you
will be my witnesses in Jerusalem and in all Judea and Samaria, and to
the end of the earth."

I've heard at least a hundred messages stressing the relevance of the Great
Commission to the calling of all of Jesus' followers. There's little disagree-
ment among Bible-believing saints: Jesus has tasked us with proclaiming
the gospel to the Church as well with making disciples by "teaching them
to observe all that I have commanded you" (Matthew 28:20).

During the Tribulation judgments described in the book of Revelation, however, we see something much different. Along with the fact that

there's no mention of the Church's presence on the earth during this time, we read of other groups functioning as the Lord's witnesses on the earth and proclaiming the gospel throughout the earth.

If we as New Testament saints are destined to endure the entire Tribulation, or even a part of it, we would expect to see references in the book of Revelation pertaining to the Church fulfilling the Great Commission during that time. We would read about members of the Body of Christ telling others about the saving message of the cross, but this isn't what God's Word says. Instead, right from the beginning of this time of wrath, the text identifies other entities who perform the task the Lord gave His Church.

Of course, there will be false Christians who meet in church buildings during this time, but the true followers of Jesus will have disappeared in the Rapture. This will necessitate the need for others to give God's message to the lost.

The Two Witnesses

The two witnesses John describes in Revelation 11:3–13 typically aren't the subject of many sermons, but they will become infamous throughout the world for forty-two months. Their notoriety during the Tribulation will no doubt arise, at least in part, from the fact that if anyone attempts to harm or kill them, fire will pour "from their mouths and consume their foes" (11:5). The Lord will also empower the pair to perform miraculous signs.

Pastor Brandon Holthaus once said people will likely regard the two witnesses as aliens from another world, given their means of defending themselves. Can you imagine the headlines these two will generate? No one will be able to harm or kill them until the end of their appointed time, when the beast will slay them.

If the Church is still present on the earth, why is it necessary for these men to appear in Jerusalem and act as God's witnesses? Didn't Jesus tell His disciples *they* were to be His "witnesses **in Jerusalem** and in all Judea and Samaria, and to the end of the earth" (Acts 1:8, emphasis added)? Today, the Church has a presence in Israel as a witness to Christ and His saving message, which, after October 7, 2023, came from believers sending money to those suffering amid the aftershock of Hamas' demonic and barbaric attack.

Something must change between now and the arrival of the Revelation 11 Jerusalem witnesses fulfilling the Church's role to do so. *The presence of these two with worldwide fame testifies that there's something strikingly different about their day and ours.* The pre-Tribulation Rapture provides the best explanation.

The apostle doesn't identify them, but many Bible commentators speculate they will be Moses and Elijah, who appeared with Jesus during His transfiguration (Matthew 17:1–5). The nature of their powers, as described in Revelation 11:6, resembles those of these Old Testament men.

People across the earth will be aware of their testimony concerning the things of the Lord. As evidence of their worldwide fame, everyone will celebrate their deaths by exchanging gifts such as we do at Christmas to celebrate Christ's birth (11:8–10). After Antichrist kills the men, their dead bodies will lie in "the street of the great city," or Jerusalem, for three and a half days. The world will rejoice over the slaying of the two, who "had been a torment to those who dwell on the earth."

This, however, isn't the end of the story. The apostle records what happens next:

> But after the three and a half days a breath of life from God entered them, and they stood up on their feet, and great fear fell on those who saw them. Then they heard a loud voice from heaven saying to them, "Come up here!" And they went up to heaven in a cloud, and their enemies watched them. (Revelation 11:11–12)

An astounded world will watch the Lord raise the men from the dead and take them up to Heaven. What a wake-up call for those alive during this time!

Perhaps the preaching of these witnesses will have a role in the repentance of the Jewish people at the end of the Tribulation. Though the earth's inhabitants will initially reject their warnings, it seems likely they will remember their words as they flee from Jerusalem after Antichrist desecrates the temple.

144,000 Sealed Jews

During the past few years, the Temple Institute in Jerusalem has located many descendants of the tribe of Levi from throughout the world. They performed this search because of their intent to train priests for the temple they plan to build.

How does this relate to Bible prophecy and the book of Revelation? Many today scoff at our literal interpretation of Revelation 7:1–8 where John records the Lord's sealing of twelve thousand Jewish men from twelve tribes of Israel. Although it's true that this mocking often comes from those who believe God has rejected Israel, they insinuate that such a rendering of this passage is impossible, therefore foolish to adhere to.

However, if a Jerusalem-based group can locate Levites all over the world, who's to doubt the Lord's ability to find the eleven other tribes of Israel? And why would the Apostle John give us so much detail about this group of 144,000 Jews if he didn't intend for us to believe God will indeed call and use just such a group for His purposes during this time?

The identification of this group as men from the twelve tribes of Israel validates the Church's absence during the Tribulation period. I make this claim for several reasons.

First, these select Jewish believers will play a key role in bringing a multitude of people to saving faith during the Tribulation. Immediately after John identifies them, he describes a scene of a throng of saints in Heaven, whom he later identifies as those who have come "out of the great tribulation" (Revelation 7:9–14). This close connection points to the participation of the 144,000 in bringing a great many people to saving faith in Jesus during the Tribulation.

Since this group performs the Great Commission assigned to the apostles and the Church, doesn't this argue for our absence during the Tribulation? If the Body of Christ were present on the earth during this time, why wouldn't the Lord seal some of its members rather than a select group of Jewish men to preach the Gospel? If, however, this is the seventieth week of Daniel with God's attention redirected to Israel, it makes perfect sense that He would task this group with preaching His word.

Although the entire world will become aware of the two witnesses in Jerusalem, it appears that their signs and message will apply primarily to Israel, since they remain in Jerusalem during their entire ministry and they seem to be Old Testament characters. The 144,000 will be the ones to take the gospel message to the nations so people might have the opportunity to hear it and believe.

Second, the very existence of this substantial number of sealed Jewish men also verifies a pre-Tribulation Rapture. Consider what Paul wrote in Colossians 3:11 about the Body of Christ: "Here there is not Greek and Jew, circumcised and uncircumcised, barbarian, Scythian, slave, free; but Christ is all, and in all."

By the time we get to Revelation 7, something has radically changed from how the apostle described the Body of Christ in this verse. Contrary to the Lord's purposes for the Church Age, a clear distinction now exists between a large group of Jewish men and other followers of Jesus.

If the Lord intended for His Church to endure the early months and years of the Tribulation, we wouldn't see a special sealing and calling of the 144,000 Jewish men to proclaim the gospel. This distinction, however, not only fits perfectly with the pre-Tribulation Rapture, but also verifies the absence of the Body of Christ during this time.

An Angel Proclaims the Gospel

The presence of an angel proclaiming the Gospel during the Tribulation also tells us that the Church Age will have already ended.

> Then I saw another angel flying directly overhead, with an eternal gospel to proclaim to those who dwell on earth, to every nation and tribe and language and people. And he said with a loud voice, "Fear God and give him glory, because the hour of his judgment has come, and worship him who made heaven and earth, the sea and the springs of water." (Revelation 14:6–7)

This is yet another confirmation of the pre-Tribulation Rapture. Why would God send an angel to fulfill the Great Commission if the Church remained present on the earth? The presence of an angel proclaiming the gospel indicates the Church must already be with the Lord in Heaven.

In Romans 10:14–17, Paul stresses the need for people to hear the "word of Christ" to arrive at saving faith. God, in His great *mercy*, will make sure that even in the midst of the worst time in human history, people will hear the message of salvation. He will give those left behind one last opportunity to turn to the Lord, and a multitude will heed His final invitation.

During this time of judgment on the earth, however, most people will reject the message of the two witnesses, the 144,000, and the angel. John records these tragic results in Revelation 9:20–21:

> The rest of mankind, who were not killed by these plagues, did not repent of the works of their hands nor give up worshiping demons and idols of gold and silver and bronze and stone and wood, which cannot see or hear or walk, nor did they repent of their murders or their sorceries or their sexual immorality or their thefts.

Despite seeing undeniable evidence of the Lord's direct intervention in the world and the presence of many witnesses to the saving message of the cross, most people will cling to their sin and reject His offer of salvation.

⋐∾ *Wisdom defends the pre-Tribulation Rapture by:*

1. Confirming our unique place as the Body of Christ and heirs to His kingdom rather than current possessors of it.
2. Verifying that the Rapture, as described in 1 Thessalonians 4:13–17, must happen if the Bible is true.
3. Demonstrating that the Rapture and Second Coming are two distinct events separated by a significant period of time.

4. Promising to keep the Body of Christ out of the Day of the Lord wrath that will suddenly fall upon the unbelieving world in the last days.

5. Providing compelling proof that we will depart from the world before the start of the Day of the Lord.

6. Assuring us that Heaven will be our destination when Jesus appears to take us home.

7. Picturing resurrected New Testament saints in Heaven, with the Lamb, before He opens the seals that initiate the Tribulation judgments. We're already there before the Tribulation starts.

8. Demonstrating the absence of the Church with the presence of others performing the tasks of the Great Commission.

Chapter 23

WATCH!

It would be impossible for Jesus to use these words ["keep watch"] in reference to His later coming in power and great glory at the end of the Great Tribulation. That even will not happen without warning. It will be preceded by numerous dramatic signs.... No person who understands the Scriptures could possibly miss those signs. Any believer who had seen these signs would expect the glorious appearing of Jesus at any moment. But here, in verse 44, Jesus tells His disciples, "the Son of Man will come at an hour when you do not expect him."[97]

—Ray C. Stedman, *What On Earth Is Happening?*

The video was unforgettable. A woman on a train remained focused on her smartphone despite scenes of destruction and fires outside her window. As she smiled at the images on her phone, she remained oblivious to the fact that only a pane of glass separated her from the devastation along the train's path.

This short clip aptly sums up modern life. Today's many distractions keep the majority of people unaware of the dangers of our fallen world. Even many saints cling to a false sense of normality and ignore warnings that the judgments and death of the Tribulation period loom in the near future.

If there ever was a time in the history of the Church to heed Jesus' admonitions in Matthew 24 and 25 (the Olivet Discourse), it's now. After He answered the disciples' questions regarding the signs that mark His "coming and the end of the age" (24:3), He gave three specific instructions that pertain to our awareness of the time in which we live:

1. "Therefore, stay awake, for you do not know on what day your Lord is coming" (Matthew 24:42).
2. "Therefore, you also must be ready, for the Son of Man is coming at an hour you do not expect" (Matthew 24:44).
3. "Watch therefore, for you know neither the day nor the hour" (Matthew 25:13).

Rather than allow the things of this life to distract us, as the woman on the train, the Lord asks us to remain watchful, knowing He might appear at any moment, even at a time we think is unlikely (24:44).

Watch for the Rapture

To understand why Jesus urges us in the Olivet Discourse to be watchful, we must determine which event He has in mind. Are we to watch for the Rapture or for His return to the earth at the end of the Tribulation?

The Lord uses two different words to describe His return to earth in Matthew 24. In verses 30 and 42, He refers to it with a term denoting His arrival at a particular destination, a word the writers of the New Testament use 643 times in this way. In verses 37 and 39, Jesus uses the familiar Greek word *parousia,* which has the basic meaning of "presence," which in Scripture not only applies to the Second Coming, but sometimes to the Rapture, such as in 2 Thessalonians 2:1.

Former pastor and author Ray C. Stedman provides helpful insight into what the word *parousia* signifies in the context of Matthew 24:

In one sense, He *is* describing one event: His *parousia,* His presence on earth. The *parousia* begins with His return to remove the church, and it climaxes with His glorious manifestation. So these two events are really different aspects of one *parousia,* one presence of the Lord Jesus Christ.

The first sentence of this section, however, makes it clear which aspect of His *parousia* the Lord is describing. At the beginning of the passage, He clearly states that His coming will be completely unpredictable: "No one knows about that day or hour, not even the angels in heaven, nor the Son, but only the Father." This description fits only one aspect of His *parousia:* The removal of the church, the Rapture.[98]

In the Olivet Discourse, the Lord is telling us to watch for His *parousia,* or His presence, which believers would first experience with the Lord's appearing. For those left behind, it will mark His unmistakable intervention in human history as He makes His *parousia* felt throughout the earth.

The Lord's command to "stay awake" suggests He has in mind an unexpected event, such as the arrival of a thief in one's home (Matthew 24:42–43; see also 1 Thessalonians 5:1–3). He instructs us to always "be ready," because the event that kicks off this time of judgment will happen at a time we "do not expect." (24:44). His words can only apply to the Rapture, which will happen when few people are anticipating it.

As discussed in earlier chapters, Christ appearing to take us home will initiate the Day of the Lord, a time of extended wrath. Of course, He's actively involved in our world at the moment; He's calling many to saving faith and restraining the appearance of Antichrist and the widespread devastation that will occur when He opens the seals of judgment (Revelation 6:1–8). Jesus' direct involvement in human affairs, however, is ever so close. First Thessalonians 5:1–3 tells us the Day of the Lord will begin with sudden destruction.

Jesus' command for us to watch for His surprising intrusion into the affairs of humanity can't possibly refer to the Second Coming, which will happen after a time of "great tribulation" on the earth (Matthew 24:21–29). His return to the earth will not catch people by surprise. By that time, most people alive at the start of the Tribulation will be dead. Among the survivors, those who refuse to repent will live in great fear of what might happen next. The few surviving saints who know and believe Bible prophecy will expect the Second Coming to occur about three and half years after Antichrist desecrates the temple (Matthew 24:15).

Jesus's warning that He will come "at an hour you do not expect" (Matthew 24:44) can only apply to the Rapture and the abrupt start of the Day of the Lord.

The simple command to "watch" carries with it the admonition to pay attention to the signs that pertain to our Lord appearing to take us home. For those who aren't believers in Christ and who are unaware of the times in which we now live, His wrath will come upon them like a "thief in the night."

The Days of Noah and the Rapture

In the context of watching for His return, the Lord compared the time leading up to His *parousia* with that of the days of Noah:

> For as were the days of Noah, so will be the coming of the Son of Man. For as in those days before the flood they were eating and drinking, marrying and giving in marriage, until the day when Noah entered the ark, and they were unaware until the flood came and swept them all away, so will be the coming of the Son of Man. (Matthew 24:37–39)

Just like in the days before the Great Flood, a sense of normalcy will prevail on the earth before the time of judgment. The people of Noah's day ignored his warnings and, as a result, they didn't know judgment was coming until the rain started to fall. Doesn't this sound like the days in which we live?

Jesus' reference to the people of Noah's day "eating and drinking, marrying and giving in marriage" depicts a normal ebb and flow of life, with nothing out of the unusual expected in the near or distant future. Until the rain began, the antediluvian people assumed God wouldn't interfere with their everyday life, much less judge their wicked ways.

Again, this must refer to Jesus appearing as described in 1 Thessalonians 4:13–5:11. By the end of the Tribulation, any sense of the status quo will have long since ended. "Marrying and giving in marriage," if even possible, will be rare events. The surviving remnant of Jews will be hiding, supernaturally protected from the beast (Revelation 12:13–17). For the few Tribulation saints who remain alive, their days will consist of fleeing from the wrath of Antichrist and scrambling to survive despite not being able to buy or sell goods and services. Life during the last half of the Tribulation will be treacherous; nothing will resemble the day in which we now live.

Jesus' parable of the "faithful and wise servant" in Matthew 24:45–51 confirms that His arrival happens during a time of relative business as usual. If the Lord has in mind His return at the end of the Tribulation after His judgments have devastated the planet, the "wicked servant" most certainly wouldn't say, "My master is delayed," and live in the reckless way the Lord describes. This picture is of routine day-to-day living that will characterize most people before the wrath of the Day of the Lord falls upon the earth after the Rapture.

In both texts regarding the start of the Day of the Lord, we see that His judgment arrives as a "thief in the night" (Matthew 24:43; 1 Thessalonians 5:2) and the Geek word *gregoreo* appears in both appeals for believers to "stay alert" or "stay awake" (24:42; 5:6). The 1 Thessalonians passage concludes with the Lord's promise to deliver us from the wrath of God that's coming (5:9–10), which is also inherent in the commands Jesus gives in the Olivet Discourse (Matthew 24 and 25).

If Jesus intended for His followers to remain watchful for His coming, we would expect to see evidence of it in the remainder of the New Testament, and that's exactly what we see.

The Matter of Imminence

In the writings of the apostles, the Lord's pleas for His followers to "watch" for His coming ignite a sense of imminence, the idea that He could appear at any moment.

Paul anticipated that he himself might even be alive at the Rapture (1 Corinthians 15:52–53; 1 Thessalonians 4:17). It wasn't until the end of his life that the Lord showed him he would face martyrdom for his faith, but even then, he pointed to the reward that would come to those who long for Jesus' appearing (2 Timothy 4:7–8).

We see further evidence of Paul's expectation of Jesus' soon appearing in Philippians 3:20–21: "But our citizenship is in heaven, and from it we await a Savior, the Lord Jesus Christ, who will transform our lowly body to be like his glorious body, by the power that enables him to subject all things to himself."

The Greek word for "await" in verse 20 points to an "intense antici-pation" or an "excited expectation" of a future event.[99] This was the same word Luke used in the original for "await" to describe Paul's restless "wait-ing" in Athens for Silas and Timothy to rejoin him (Acts 17:16). After the apostle's distressing experiences in Philippi, Thessalonica, and Berea, we know he intently watched and longed for a reunion with his fellow laborers.

Dr. Ron Rhodes sums up the matter of imminence this way:

> The term *imminent* means "ready to take place" or "impending." The New Testament teaches that the rapture is imminent—that is, there is nothing that must be prophetically fulfilled before the rapture occurs (see 1 Corinthians 1:7; 16:22; Philippians 3:20; 4:5; 1 Thessalonians 1:10; Titus 2:13; Hebrews 9:28; James 5:7–9; 1 Peter 1:13; Jude 21). The rapture is a signless event that can occur at any moment. This contrasts with the second coming of Christ, which is preceded by seven years of signs in the tribula-tion period (Revelation 6–18).[100]

Did you know believers in the early centuries copied Paul's prayer in 1 Corinthians 16:22: "Our Lord, come." In the original, the word is the Aramaic *maranatha*, which signifies "a petition to Christ that He should return now—at any moment. Paul used it in this letter to Greek-speak-ing (mostly Gentile) Christians in Corinth because it expressed an idea that had become universal in the early church. Christ could come at any moment, and Christians called upon him to do so."[101]

Why would the early followers of Jesus pray for Him to come if they didn't believe it could occur in their lifetime? *This prayer speaks to the imminent hope they cherished for His appearing.*

Do you see how the matter of imminence fits with Jesus' instructions in Matthew 24:36–51? There's coming a day, one that will happen with no warning whatsoever, when the world will feel Jesus' presence through the outpouring of His wrath upon the wicked of the earth. His unexpected direct intervention in our world will happen suddenly and will catch many unaware, just as Paul wrote in 1 Thessalonians 5:1–3.

Today, those watching for Jesus to appear know the time is exceedingly near. We see an abundance of signs telling us the events of Revelation 6 are right at the door, just about to happen. Everything is falling into place for Antichrist to control all the buying and selling throughout the entire world as depicted in Revelation 13:16–18. The technology to do this is already here, but at the midpoint of the Tribulation he will have everything at his fingertips to make it happen.

Just like Noah, we believe God's Word. We know a time of judgment is coming for the world, although those around us have no clue just how close we are to that time. Noah obeyed the Lord by building a huge ark, which would save not only a few from his family, but also a great many animals. In the same way, we obey the Lord by watching and warning others of the nearing Rapture.

Although many will continue to ridicule our belief in Jesus' soon appearing, the Bible says the Lord will reward our obedience in this regard. Shortly before his death, Paul wrote about a crown those who long for Jesus to appear will receive: "Henceforth there is laid up for me the crown of righteousness, which the Lord, the righteous judge, will award to me on that day, and not only to me but also to all who have loved his appearing" (2 Timothy 4:8).

I believe the Lord also had this crown in mind as He encouraged us, through His letter to the church at Philadelphia, to keep watching for His return: "I am coming soon. Hold fast what you have, so that no one may seize your crown" (Revelation 3:11).

Those who are truly born again will go to Heaven with Jesus when He comes for His Church. He will not leave behind the saints who are unaware of the time in which they live or even fellow believers who now ridicule our anticipation of His imminent appearing. If you are born again, you will meet your Savior in the air. No exceptions!

What, then, is the benefit of watching and anticipating His appearing? Those who understand the times in which we live and yearn for His appearing will receive special recognition at the judgment seat of Christ. I'm convinced that pastors who teach what the Bible says about the end times and encourage their flock to watch for Jesus to appear soon will be among those rewarded for their obedience.

ᘓᕽ *Wisdom defends the pre-Tribulation Rapture by:*

1. Confirming our unique place as the Body of Christ and heirs to His kingdom rather than current possessors of it.

2. Verifying that the Rapture, as described in 1 Thessalonians 4:13–17, must happen if the Bible is true.

3. Demonstrating that the Rapture and Second Coming are two distinct events separated by a significant period of time.

4. Promising to keep the Body of Christ out of the Day of the Lord wrath that will suddenly fall upon the unbelieving world in the last days.

5. Providing compelling proof that we will depart from the world before the start of the Day of the Lord.

6. Assuring us that Heaven will be our destination when Jesus appears to take us home.

7. Picturing resurrected New Testament saints in Heaven, with the Lamb, before He opens the seals that initiate the Tribulation judgments. We're already there before the Tribulation starts.

8. Demonstrating the absence of the Church with the presence of others performing the tasks of the Great Commission.

9. Instructing us to watch for Jesus' return, the Rapture, more than we do for any other prophetic event.

Chapter 24

PICTURES
OF THE RAPTURE

The Bible pictures the Rapture as an event when a bridegroom comes for his bride. Both Jesus and the Apostle Paul spoke of the Rapture in terms that would have sparked images of first-century AD Jewish weddings, especially to those in Galilee, home to Jesus and His disciples.

As we look at these ancient customs, we see a picture that not only washes away our fears regarding Rapture, but also makes passages such as John 14:2–3 and 1 Thessalonians 4:13–18 come alive with a joyous anticipation of meeting our Savior in the air![102]

—Jonathan C. Brentner, *The Triumph of the Redeemed*

O ur first line of defense for the pre-Tribulation appearing of Jesus rests on the words of Scripture. In the preceding chapters, I've presented compelling evidence confirming the biblical necessity of the Tribulation period, the Lord's restoration of a kingdom to Israel, and the placing of Jesus' return for His Church at the start of the Day of the Lord, before the seven-year time of Jacob's trouble begins.

We examined why there must be something we call the "Rapture." The term refers to a specific order of events clearly defined in passages such as 1 Thessalonians 4:13–5:11 and 1 Corinthians 15:47–55. Those of us who say there will be a Rapture are simply saying we believe the events of these passages and others will happen in the future because, as of yet, they clearly have not taken place.

In 1 Thessalonians 4:17, the Greek word for the catching up of saints to meet the Lord in the air is *harpazo*. The word signifies seizing something by force in order to claim it for oneself. It carries the connotation of being caught up and carried to another place, which is what will happen at the time of the Rapture.

Although the world has never seen anything of the magnitude of what will take place when Jesus suddenly catches up hundreds of millions of His followers to meet Him in the air, similar events appear on the pages of God's Word.

Biblical Examples

The story of Enoch gives us the first type (foreshadowing) of the Rapture. Genesis 5:24 says, "Enoch walked with God, and he was not, for God took him." He simply disappeared, which make me wonder if others witnessed it. The writer of the book of Hebrews adds the following to the account:

> By faith Enoch was taken up so that he should not see death, and he was not found, because God had taken him. Now before he was taken he was commended as having pleased God. (11:5).

The Lord removed this ancient saint from the earth before his death and "took him" up to be with Him in Heaven. This is what will happen to the living saints at the moment of the Rapture. After Jesus transforms our bodies into ones like His, He will catch us up to meet Him in the air just as Paul explained in 1 Thessalonians 4:17. Just like Enoch, we will disappear.

Although the story of Elijah differs from the New Testament Rapture texts, it provides us with an example of the Lord directly transporting someone from earth to glory. We find the description of what happened in 2 Kings 2:11–12:

> And as they still went on and talked, behold, chariots of fire and horses of fire separated the two of them. And Elijah went up by a whirlwind into heaven. And Elisha saw it and he cried, "My

father, my father! The chariots of Israel and its horsemen!" And he saw him no more.

The above incident reminds me of Jesus' response to the Sadducees who sought to disprove the resurrection of the dead. He told them they knew "neither the Scriptures nor the power of God" (Matthew 22:29). The God who is able to send chariots of fire to take Elijah into the sky is most certainly able to transform our bodies into immortal ones and take us to Heaven.

Something similar to the Rapture happened to Philip after he baptized the Ethiopian eunuch. Luke recorded the incident for us in Acts 8:39–40:

> When they came up out of the water, the Spirit of the Lord snatched Philip away, and the eunuch no longer saw him, but went on his way rejoicing. But Philip found himself at Azotus, and as he passed through he kept proclaiming the gospel to all the cities until he came to Caesarea. (LSB)

In verse 39, Luke used same Greek word, *harpazo*, that Paul used for the Lord catching us up to meet Him in the air (1 Thessalonians 4:17). With Philip, the Lord didn't snatch him up to Heaven, but transported him to another location.

In 2 Corinthians 12:1–5, Paul recounts his experience of being "caught up to the third heaven." Here we see the word *harpazo* in the apostle's story of the Lord grabbing him from earth and taking him to Heaven.

These accounts illustrate what will happen when Jesus comes for us. He will quickly lift us up to meet Him and, in an instant, we will be in glory with Him.

"Come Up Here!"

Two times in the book of Revelation, a voice from Heaven proclaims, "Come up here!" In both instances, we see a picture of the Rapture.

216

The first instance appears in Revelation 4:1–2, which follows Jesus' letters to the seven churches. It's clear that the intent of His messages to them go far beyond the late first century AD to include the entire Church Age. In three of His addresses, He refers either to His future kingdom or His Coming (Revelation 2:26–27, 3:10–11, 21).

Notice John's words as he transitions to the scene where he will see the twenty-four elders who represent the Church in Heaven:

> After these things I looked, and behold, a door standing open in heaven, and the first voice which I had heard, like the sound of a trumpet speaking with me, said, "Come up here, and I will show you what must take place after these things." Immediately I was in the Spirit, and behold, a throne was standing in heaven, and One sitting on the throne. (Revelation 4:1–2)

Is this not a picture of the Rapture? In language reminiscent of 1 Thessalonians 4:16–17, John hears a voice calling him upward. Someday we will also hear a shout and the sound of a trumpet, and we'll suddenly find ourselves in glory with imperishable bodies. We know this to be true from the words recorded earlier in the New Testament. John's experience pictures what will happen to us in the future.

Next, we return to the two witnesses and what the apostle sees concerning their ministry on the earth. They will also hear a voice from Heaven bidding them to "come up here":

> But after the three and a half days, the breath of life from God came into them, and they stood on their feet, and great fear fell upon those who were watching them. And they heard a loud voice from heaven saying to them, "Come up here." Then they went up into heaven in the cloud, and their enemies watched them. (Revelation 11:11–12)

Of course, the details differ from what we will experience when Jesus comes for us. This passage does provide, however, an additional picture of the Lord taking people from earth up to Heaven. In this case, the Lord raises them from the dead for the entire world to see and then brings them up to Himself.

Galilean Wedding Customs

In two of my previous books, I address how the Jewish wedding customs of the first century AD not only portray the Rapture, but they also confirm our understanding of it. In 2020, a documentary titled *Before the Wrath* provided a picture of the Galilean marriages of Jesus' day. Some of Jesus' words and actions in the Upper Room the night before He died upon the cross relate to these practices, which the disciples would have witnessed in their hometowns.

I return briefly to this topic because Jesus' words to describe His return for the Church come directly from the marriage traditions of His day, particularly those pertaining to the relationship between the groom and bride. They give us a compelling illustration of the pre-Tribulation Rapture; one Jesus' disciples would've understood.

The following paragraphs come from what I wrote in *Hereafter*. I include them here because the wedding customs of ancient Galilee provide further illumination to the role of Jesus as the Bridegroom of the Church and provide much insight into His return to take us back to Heaven.

> First-century AD Galilean marriages began with a betrothal ceremony witnessed by the parents of the couple and several people from the town in which they lived. The man formally proposed by offering the woman he wanted to marry a cup of wine. She signified her willingness to become his wife by accepting and drinking from the cup; she indicated her unwillingness to marry him by refusing the cup. If she accepted, her future husband took the cup back and also drank the wine, sealing their marital covenant.
>
> The disciples witnessed this custom again in the Upper Room during the Lord's Supper, when Jesus spoke the following words, as recorded in Matthew 26:27–29:

"And he took the cup, and gave thanks, and gave it to them, saying, Drink ye all of it; For this is my blood of the new testament, which is shed for many for the remission of sins. But I say unto you, I will not drink henceforth of this fruit of the vine, until that day when I drink it new with you in my Father's kingdom."

The disciples surely caught the double meaning. Not only was the Lord including them in the New Covenant promised to Israel, but in offering them the cup of wine, He was, in essence, "proposing marriage" to the Church. The disciples accepted His proposal on our behalf by drinking from the cup before they passed it back to Jesus.

In ancient Galilee, after the groom confirmed the betrothal, he stated that he wouldn't again drink wine until the couple's wedding feast. Jesus' identical promise that night in the Upper Room likely further stirred the disciples' memories of betrothal ceremonies they had witnessed (Matthew 26:29). Jesus was acting as a prospective Bridegroom of the Church, His future Bride.

With the binding marriage covenant between the man and woman in place, the groom left to prepare a room for the couple in his father's house, their future residence. The groom typically announced his intention to do so at the end of the betrothal ceremony.

When Jesus told His disciples that He was leaving to "prepare a place" for them in His "Father's house" (John 14:2–3), they would have instantly related His words to this custom. He was leaving to prepare a home for them in Heaven, just as the Jewish bridegrooms did on earth. The image of houses in Galilee with one or more such additions probably came to their minds. They knew what Jesus meant.

With the completion of the bridal chamber, the father of the groom determined its readiness and decided when to send his son to fetch his bride. Jesus twice alluded to the fact that the timing of His appearing to take us to glory, which would set off the Day of the Lord judgments, rests with the Father (Matthew 24:36; Acts 1:7).

In Jesus' day, the groom most often went to retrieve his bride in the middle of the night and amid much fanfare:

The bridegroom would abduct his bride secretly, like a thief at night, and take her to the wedding chamber. As the bridegroom approached the bride's home, he would shout and blow the shofar (ram's horn trumpet) so that she had some warning to gather her belongings to take into the wedding chamber. The bridegroom and his friends would come into the bride's house and get the bride and her bridesmaids.

Although the bride didn't know exactly when the groom would arrive, she recognized when the time was near. Once she and her bridesmaids heard the noisy procession heading their way, they emerged from her house to greet the groom and his friends.

The bride then stepped into a litter (a kind of portable couch mounted on poles), and those accompanying the groom would lift her off the ground and carry her to the home of the groom. Just like the Jewish brides of the first century, when Jesus comes for us, His Bride, He will carry us to His Father's house in Heaven. The similarities are remarkable and unmistakable.

Brides of Jesus' day longed for the day their grooms would appear and take them back to their fathers' house. If someone had written a romance novel back then, this would've been the high point of the love story. For us, the Rapture marks the culmination of an even grander love story, that of Jesus coming for His Bride, the Church, the one for whom He gave His life on the cross to redeem. His appearing will be an equally joyous event as He quickly replaces our surprise with tears of ecstasy.[103]

This picture dovetails perfectly with all that the New Testament tells us about the Rapture. Apart from the words of the various texts supporting it, the Jewish wedding customs would not prove a pre-Tribulation

Rapture. However, because they fit together so well, the first century AD Galilean rituals help us understand Jesus' words in the Upper Room and provide amazing comfort for what lies ahead.

☙ *Wisdom defends the pre-Tribulation Rapture by:*

1. Confirming our unique place as the Body of Christ and heirs to His kingdom rather than current possessors of it.

2. Verifying that the Rapture, as described in 1 Thessalonians 4:13–17, must happen if the Bible is true.

3. Demonstrating that the Rapture and Second Coming are two distinct events separated by a significant period of time.

4. Promising to keep the Body of Christ out of the Day of the Lord wrath that will suddenly fall upon the unbelieving world in the last days.

5. Providing compelling proof that we will depart from the world before the start of the Day of the Lord.

6. Assuring us that Heaven will be our destination when Jesus appears to take us home.

7. Picturing resurrected New Testament saints in Heaven, with the Lamb, before He opens the seals that initiate the Tribulation judgments. We're already there before the Tribulation starts.

8. Demonstrating the absence of the Church with the presence of others performing the tasks of the Great Commission.

9. Instructing us to watch for Jesus' return, the Rapture, more than for any other prophetic event.

10. Providing examples of the Rapture and picturing it in such a way that points us directly to its occurrence before the wrath of the Day of the Lord.

Chapter 25

THE RAPTURE:
FREQUENTLY ASKED QUESTIONS

The rapture question, while neglected by modern liberals, is one of the main areas in dispute in conservative eschatology. The Scriptures predict that the church will be raptured, or "caught up" to heaven, at the coming of the Lord for them. The word *rapture* is from *rapere,* found in the expression "caught up" in the Latin translation of 1 Thessalonians 4:17. If this is a literal, future event, it is a most important aspect of the hope of the church.[104]

—John F. Walvoord, *The Rapture Question*

Throughout this book, I have sought to supply convincing biblical evidence leading to the sound doctrine of the pre-Tribulation Rapture. As a way to summarize the reasons supporting it, as well as answer any lingering questions, I'll address several frequently asked questions regarding our hope in Jesus' appearing.

It's also my hope that the answers will resolve any remaining concerns you have and provide you with answers for those who scoff at our anticipation of the Lord's appearing.

Q. Is there a biblical basis for the Rapture?

A. Absolutely. Although the word "Rapture" doesn't appear in our English translations of the New Testament, for the past four hundred years, students of Bible prophecy have used the term to designate what the apostles describe in passages such as 1 Thessalonians 4:13–5:10; 1

Corinthians 15:47–55; Titus 2:13; Philippians 3:20–21, James 5:8; and 1 John 3:2–3. Jesus Himself referred to this event in John 14:2–3 and Revelation 3:10–11a.

Ed Hindson sums up the matter perfectly in his book, *Future Glory:*

> The truth of the Bible is there *must* be a rapture. There must be a catching up. There must be a time when dead believers are raised, and the living are caught up into the presence of God. If somebody doesn't believe in the pretribulational rapture, they should not go around saying, "well I don't believe there is ever going to be a rapture." They simply don't agree with the *timing* of the event. The fact of the rapture is clear in the Bible.[105]

To say there is no Rapture is to question the reliability of the entire Scripture. The New Testament confirms that there will be such an event regardless of where we place it in relation to the Tribulation period. How can one deny it without calling into question the integrity of God's Word?

Q. How does belief in a pre-Tribulation Rapture align with the three key tests of biblical wisdom?

A. Our expectation of Jesus' imminent appearing closely aligns with the three aspects of biblical wisdom identified in the introduction.

The words of the New Testament point to an event that's far different than Jesus' Second Coming and must happen before it to allow time for people to come to saving faith in Jesus, survive the Tribulation, and enter the Millennium in natural bodies. Paul's assurances to the Thessalonian believers concerning the Day of the Lord, along with Jesus' promises, provide ample evidence that the Rapture must happen before the seventieth week of Daniel.

Our expectation of Jesus' imminent appearing keeps our focus on Him and exalts His place in our lives. John's description of the Rapture places Him at the center of our hope (1 John 3:2–3). In all the passages related to His return for us, the focus is on Jesus and Him alone. He is the substance of our hope (see Philippians 3:20–21). Notice the emphasis on our Savior in Paul's description of His return for us: "When Christ who is your life appears, then you also will appear with him in glory" (Colossians 3:4).

Lastly, isn't it just like the Father to keep His own safe from His judgments? Noah and his family survived the Flood because of the ark the Lord commanded him to build. The presence of other witnesses on the earth after our departure also fits with what we know of His nature to provide yet another opportunity for people to come to saving faith in His Son. Even in the midst of pouring out His wrath on the earth, people will hear the good news via the 144,000 sealed Jews and the angel who will proclaim it to the nations.

Q. Did the doctrine of the Rapture originate with John Darby?

A. Absolutely not! Those who maintain the lie that John Darby originated the idea of the Rapture deceive a great many believers.

The use of "Rapture" to depict what the apostle described in 1 Thessalonians 4:17 goes back almost four hundred years. In 1627, English Bible commentator Joseph Mede (1586–1639) "used the word 'rapture' six times, all in reference to the saints meeting the Lord in the air."[106] There's a long history of Bible scholars using the word "rapture" in regard to Jesus' appearing to take us back to Heaven.

During the 1740s, another Bible commentator, John Gill, wrote:

> Suddenly, in a moment, in the twinkling of an eye, and with force and power...and to which rapture will contribute, the agility which the bodies of the raised and the changed saints will have and this rapture of the living saints will be together with them.[107]

Several theologians in the early centuries of the Church believed there would be a lengthy time of tribulation on the earth between Jesus taking His saints out of the world and the Second Coming.

As noted in chapter 21, Cyprian, a bishop in the city of Carthage during the third century AD, believed the Lord would remove His Church before a time of catastrophes on the earth. Ephraim the Syrian (AD 306–373), in a sermon entitled "On the Last Times, the Antichrist, and the End of the World," clearly asserted a belief in a pre-Tribulation Rapture.[108]

Let me be very candid. If someone insists the doctrine of the pre-Tribulation Rapture originated with John Darby, they are either very much ill-informed or attempting to deceive you. Not only does the New Testament teach that there must be a Rapture, but many throughout the history of the Church believed Jesus would come for His saints before a time of Tribulation that would happen on the earth prior to His Second Coming.

Q. Will the Rapture be secret?

A. Many critics state that we're wrong for our belief in a "secret Rapture" because it's unbiblical. While only believers will experience it, the entire world will feel its impact. This will be one of the most dramatic events ever to occur on planet earth. In that sense, I'm always confused when people refer to as "secret."

In America, the sudden disappearance of tens of millions will have a dramatic effect on all areas of life, with widespread chaos ensuing long afterward. The same will be true in many other parts of the world. This will mark the beginning of the Lord's direct intervention in the world, and people will notice it.

Those who attach the word "secret" to our hope are simply seeking to add a negative connotation. For us, it will be an utterly joyous occurrence. For those left behind, it will be a nightmare.

Q. Will the Lord leave behind any of His saints?

A. When the Lord appears, He will take all those who are truly born again back to Heaven with Him. He will not leave behind any saint to endure the ravages of the Day of the Lord.

All those who have died in Christ will come out of their graves with resurrected bodies. As for the living, everyone who belongs to Him will suddenly find themselves in glory. Rewards will vary for faithfulness and service. Those who are watching for His appearance will receive a special crown. However, the Lord will not leave even one of His saints behind at the time of the Rapture.

The suggestion that somehow the behavior of believers will be a factor in who Jesus takes at the time of His appearing contradicts the words of Ephesians of 2:8–9. If works have absolutely no role in our salvation, how can they possibly factor into its culmination (Romans 8:23–25)?

If Ephesians 1:3–14 represents our eternal standing as redeemed saints, and it does, then it's out of the question that Jesus would leave any regenerated and justified saint behind at His appearing. What separation can possibly exist between all those who "have become the righteousness of God" in Christ (2 Corinthians 5:21)?

Q. What will happen before the Rapture?

A. The Rapture will be a signless event; in other words, the Bible doesn't list anything as needing to occur before we hear the shout and the blare of the trumpet. It's imminent; it can happen at any moment.

As someone who has watched for Jesus' appearing for many years, I didn't anticipate that I would see as much being set up for the judgments of Revelation 6 and the mark of the beast as we witness today. I'm convinced Jesus is coming for us soon, perhaps even today, but we may see evil and lawlessness become much more prevalent before He takes us out of here.

Q. If I'm alive at the time, what will I experience when Jesus appears?

A. In 1 Thessalonians 4:16, Paul writes that "the Lord himself will descend from heaven with a cry of command, with the voice of an archangel, and with the sound of the trumpet of God." Almost simultaneous with hearing these things, He will change our lowly bodies "to be like his glorious body" (Philippians 3:21; see also 1 Corinthians 15:51–55).

Because of the instantaneous nature of the Rapture, it's not possible to say what we will hear or feel in the moment. We may hear the shout and the sound of the trumpet a split second before we meet the Lord in the air. Although it might cause an initial surge of fear, our instant transformation will quickly alleviate any anxiety we might possibly sense.

The Bible assures us that Jesus will bring us to glory, to His Father's house in Heaven (John 14:2–3; Colossians 3:4). I believe our immediate transformation will preclude any fear we might have. Even if we're startled, the outcome will be so wondrous that we will soon forget its sudden interruption into our lives. If you have a fear of heights like me, that will disappear at the moment the Rapture begins.

Q. Why should we believe in something that gives believers in America an unfair advantage over those who are persecuted throughout the world?

A. I was in seminary when I first heard someone object to the pre-Tribulation Rapture on the basis that American followers of Jesus must suffer like those throughout the world. Because of that, the objection went, we must endure the Tribulation. This is wrong on many levels.

First, all we believe pertaining to matters of faith must come from the words of Scripture, not from our experience. This argument ignores the strong evidence from the New Testament that places Jesus' appearance before the Tribulation. So much error in the Church comes as the result of people interpreting key passages of the Bible based upon what they think is right or what they encounter.

Second, different levels of persecution existed among the churches Jesus addressed in Revelation 2–3. Believers in Smyrna faced deadly opposition for their faith, while the Lord promised to deliver the saints at Philadelphia from the "hour of testing." The same is true in church history. In fact, today is the worst time of deadly persecution in terms of those martyred for their faith. The Bible assures us of opposition to our faith, but it doesn't say everyone will experience martyrdom.

Third, we must acknowledge the Lord's sovereignty in such matters. Believers in my parents' generation, all of whom are already with the Lord, never experienced the opposition to their faith that currently exists in the US. The Lord spared them, but, depending on how soon the Rapture occurs, we may face deadly persecution here as well.

The timing of the Rapture has nothing to do with the experience of believers in America—or anywhere else, for that matter.

Q. How can I be ready for the Rapture?

A. If you know the Lord Jesus as your Savior, you will go to Heaven with Jesus when He appears. Jesus secured the reservation for our trip to Glory by the blood He shed on the cross as payment for our sins. At the time of our rebirth, God pronounces us righteous, and nothing can change His decree.

You are ready for the Rapture the moment you come to saving faith in Jesus. He will not leave you behind.

In 2 Timothy 4:8, Paul wrote about a special "crown of righteousness" the Lord will someday award to those who love "his appearing." Though the Lord will not leave the others behind, the wise watch for His appearing and live in eager anticipation of it.

Q. How might I answer someone who tells me the Rapture is all about scaring people?

A. The best response to such criticism is to point out the many blessings that will come our way when Jesus appears to take us home. He will resurrect all our loved ones who have died in Christ and then catch us up in the air with them. He will give all of us immortal and sinless bodies that will never again get sick, suffer the impacts of aging, or die. We will live forever with Him in sinless perfection. These future realities keep me longing for the Rapture.

Jesus is also preparing a place for us in Heaven. Imagine the wonder of seeing our new forever home in the New Jerusalem.

Of course, the prospect of life on earth suddenly ending adds uncertainty to what lies ahead. We can know, however, that Jesus will make the transition smooth. Once in Glory, we will not feel the tiniest desire to go back to our former lives.

As our time on the earth becomes all the more foreboding, we will welcome the escape from the terrors ahead in the near future.

ℰ *Wisdom defends the pre-Tribulation Rapture by:*

1. Confirming our unique place as the Body of Christ and heirs to His kingdom rather than current possessors of it.

2. Verifying that the Rapture, as described in 1 Thessalonians 4:13–17, must happen if the Bible is true.

3. Demonstrating that the Rapture and Second Coming are two distinct events separated by a significant period of time.

4. Promising to keep the Body of Christ out of the Day of the Lord wrath that will suddenly fall upon the unbelieving world in the last days.

5. Providing compelling proof that we will depart from the world before the start of the Day of the Lord.

6. Assuring us that Heaven will be our destination when Jesus appears to take us home.

7. Picturing resurrected New Testament saints in Heaven, with the Lamb, before He opens the seals that initiate the Tribulation judgments. We're already there before the Tribulation starts.

8. Demonstrating the absence of the Church with the presence of others performing the tasks of the Great Commission.

9. Instructing us to watch for Jesus' return, the Rapture, rather than any other prophetic event.

10. Providing examples of the Rapture and picturing it in such a way that points us directly to its occurrence before the wrath of the Day of the Lord.

11. Increasing our understanding of it based on what Scripture says rather than on the opinions of others.

EXALTING JESUS' NAME

It is going to be different when He returns. The first time He came as a gentle and helpless baby. He is going to return as a mighty warrior. He came the first time as a suffering lamb to die for the sins of the world, but He will return as a conquering lion who will pour out the wrath of God on those who have rejected the love, mercy and grace of God. His first coming was marked by compassion, humility, and a willingness to be judged and to die. He will return in triumph and in wrath to judge and make war against the enemies of God. He came the first time as a Servant; He is returning as a Monarch.[109]

Dr. David Reagan, *Six Reasons Why Every Christian Should Desire the Soon Return of Jesus*

All of Scripture exalts Jesus' Name. He is the personification of Wisdom in the Proverbs. Throughout the Psalms, we catch glimpses of His majestic return to the earth and righteous rule over the nations. From the first verse to the last, the book of Revelation magnifies the Lord as the Head of His Church, the Lamb breaking the seals on His title deed to the kingdoms of the world, His spectacular and magnificent return to earth, His thousand-year reign over the nations, and the inauguration of the eternal state that flows from His defeat of death and the putting of all things into "subjection under him" (1 Corinthians 15:26–28).

Wisdom's defense of Bible prophecy is, at its heart, an acclamation of the coming day the Apostle Paul wrote about in Philippians 2:9–11:

Therefore God has highly exalted him and bestowed on him the name that is above every name, so that at the name of Jesus every knee should bow, in heaven and on earth and under the earth, and every tongue confess that Jesus Christ is Lord, to the glory of God the Father.

The entire world will someday witness the Father's exaltation of His Son. They will see it in His kingdom when all nations and peoples on earth will worship and obey Him. All those who spurned His Name during their time on earth will bow their knee before Him confessing His deity.

Although the text of Colossians 1:15–20 doesn't directly speak to the matter of Bible prophecy, I believe it verifies the basic tenets of pre-millennialism. Jesus' direct intervention in the world at the beginning of the Day of the Lord with the Rapture and judgment on the nations is exactly what we might expect from the New Testament picture of His magnificence.

It's an anthem that began long ago with the Lord's revelation of it to Enoch (Jude 14–15). Throughout the Psalms, the coming of the Messiah is more than prophecies about His death on the cross, although that was necessary to redeem the lost. Like a crescendo in a thrilling musical overture, the glories of Jesus' return to earth builds throughout the Psalms and into the prophets who tell of the glories of His kingdom and the restoration of Israel.

All of Scripture builds to the grand climax of human history when Jesus, the Word of God, rides victoriously back to earth, destroys the armies of the earth arrayed against Him, and establishes His thousand-year rule over the nations (Revelation 19:11–20:6). And, wonder of wonders, we as New Testament saints will experience the jubilant praise in Heaven that will precede His return (Revelation 19:1–10), and we will ride on white horses back to the earth, with Jesus in the lead. Words fail to express the thrill we will feel at this moment.

All the end-time scenarios proposed by Replacement Theology and its offshoots twist the words of Scripture so as to unduly elevate the Church and diminish Jesus' role as the object of our hope and the One who will ultimately defeat sin and death. God's Word paints a far different ending to human history than those who adhere to theologies that seriously minimize the centrality of Christ's Second Coming or claim that it already happened.

Words of Wisdom

For me, the words of Proverbs 9 have become a beacon light illuminating my path to the glories of Jesus' millennial rule over the nations. The choice between Wisdom and Folly is, among other things, a matter of believing what the Bible says about Jesus' future rule over the kingdoms versus accepting the meager picture of it offered by those who adhere to Replacement Theology and the many other false systems of belief that have flowed from it.

These words might seem particularly harsh, especially if they're taken out of the context of the case I present throughout this book. This isn't something I would've dared to say several years ago, but it's become my inescapable conclusion after reading through the book of Proverbs each month for the past several decades. Premillennialism aligns with the wisdom that comes from careful consideration of the words in our Bibles.

No one who believes in the inspiration and inerrancy of Scripture would disagree with my assertion regarding the importance of words and what they communicate it to us. Yet when it comes to Bible prophecy, those who deny Israel's restoration as a kingdom allow human understanding to skew the meaning of words away from what the authors intended at the time they wrote. Subjective reasoning becomes the standard of interpreting what God's Word says about Israel and the end times rather than the words the Lord inspired its authors to write. They retrofit the texts to fit their preconceived ideas.

The Reformers made the same grievous error. Although their principles of Bible interpretation would lead to the revival of premillennialism in the decades that followed, they allow their hatred for the Jewish people and the remaining vestiges of Platonism to influence their view of the promised Millennium. To make their theology fit their errant view of the material world, they followed the course set by Augustine and made passages pertaining to Bible prophecy subject to their own wisdom, rather than vice versa.

Bread and Water Versus Wisdom's Feast

The exaltation of Jesus throughout the last book of the Bible brings me back to Proverbs 9 and the stark difference of the invitation Wisdom extends versus the bread and water offered by the woman Folly.

Consider the choice offered by the two in terms of the way one interprets the words of Revelation.

	Futuristic and Literal	Historic, Symbolic, and Fulfilled Prophecy
The Kingdom	We are heirs to a future glorious realm.	The Church is the kingdom; we already possess it in its fullness.
Expectation	Jesus will appear before the Tribulation, when He gives all New Testament saints immortal, glorified bodies.	The expectation is most likely death, because Jesus doesn't intervene in the world until the far-distant end of the age.
The Tribulation	We are in Heaven with Jesus during this terrible time on the earth.	It's either symbolic, fulfilled, or descriptive of our day.
Jubilant Praise and Celebration (Revelation 19)	We will experience the over-the-top wonders of this time.	This praise and celebration are either symbolic or already fulfilled.
Marriage Supper of the Lamb	This is a feast we will enjoy in Heaven with the Savior.	Such a carnal banquet is unspiritual
Second Coming	We will ride back to earth following the Lord; we are all seated on white horses.	This either already happened in AD 70, or our inclusion in it consists of meeting Jesus in the air as He returns.

	Futuristic and Literal	**Historic, Symbolic, and Fulfilled Prophecy**
Jesus' Thousand-Year Rule over the Nations	We will reign with Jesus with a level of authority based on our faithfulness in this life.	We are already reigning with Jesus, having already inherited the kingdom at our rebirth.
The New Jerusalem	This is where Jesus is preparing a place for us and will take us there when He appears. This city will be our residence for all eternity.	This is our eternal home, but we will not see it until after the end of the age when Jesus returns to earth.

In the "Futuristic and Literal" column, we see the lavish feast offered by Wisdom. Regardless of what we experience in this life, such anticipation fills us with joyful expectations of what lies ahead. The words of Romans 8:18 come to mind: "For I consider that the sufferings of this present time are not worth comparing with the glory that is to be revealed to us."

I can't think of anyone who suffered more for the cause of Christ than the Apostle Paul. Yet even for him, his current afflictions paled in significance because of His hope in Jesus' appearing.

The last column represents a summary of beliefs for those who jettison the historical-grammatical method of biblical interpretation when it comes to future things. They follow the paths of theologians who rejected the intent of the authors of prophecy in favor of what they believed about what should happen to Israel.

When I read Proverbs 9, the stark differences between premillennialism and Replacement Theology leap off the page. Regardless of the pain we experience in this life, Wisdom offers an extravagant banquet with words that depict an eternity far better than we can imagine. In comparison, the future offered by those who dismiss the glorious picture for us depicted in Revelation can only offer us bread and water.

One offers meager provisions, while the other, a joyous and jubilant celebration amid a lavish feast.

My study of the Proverbs, particularly chapters 8 and 9, along with the many Psalms that speak to the wrath of the Day of the Lord as well as the glories of His kingdom, has led me to the following observations concerning how we must apply biblical wisdom to matters pertaining to prophecy:

1. The words of Scripture matter. If we ignore the intent of its authors, we all too soon find ourselves subject to what others believe the words should mean based on their own wisdom.
2. Our beliefs about future things must align with what God's Word reveals about His character. Because He is holy, He must restore to Israel all the Land He promised—in a way that far exceeds any events of that nation's past.
3. Premillennial beliefs not only spring from the words of the Bible, but they also envision Jesus' future exaltation that aligns with Paul's proclamation of His preeminence.

These three aspects of biblical wisdom verify that the basics of pre-millennialism and confirm what we believe about the pre-Tribulation Rapture. Their unifying theme is the exaltation of Jesus' Name.

ENDNOTES

1   Daniel J. Ebert IV, *The Wisdom of God*, an essay on the Gospel Coalition Website: https://www.thegospelcoalition.org/essay/the-wisdom-of-god/.

2   Ron Rhodes, *Bible Prophecy under Siege* (Eugene, OR: Harvest House, 2024), p. 10.

3   These points come from Andy Woods, "Dispensational Hermeneutics: The Grammatico -Historical Method," at: https://www.spiritandtruth.org/teaching/documents /articles/25/25.htm?x=x#sdfootnote3sym.

4   Rhodes, *Bible Prophecy under Siege*, p. 71.

5   Bernard Ramm, *Protestant Biblical Interpretation* (Grand Rapids: Baker Book House, 1970), p. 128.

6   Don Stewart, "What Is the Doctrine of Biblical Inerrancy?" July 18, 2018, on the Blue Letter Bible website: https://www.blueletterbible.org/Comm/stewart_don/faq /bible-difficulties/question1-what-is-the-doctrine-of-biblical-inerrancy.cfm.

7   Quote taken from a Harbinger's Daily article, "Reading Israel out of Biblical Prophecy: The Crafty Playbook of Replacement Theology, published on September 15, 2024, at: https://harbingersdaily.com/reading-israel-out-of-biblical-prophecy-the-crafty-playbook -of-replacement-theology/.

8   The full statement can be found at: https://www.thegospelcoalition.org/themelios /article/the-chicago-statement-on-biblical-inerrancy/.

9   Ibid.

10 Quote of Stanley from the Relevant website: https://relevantmagazine.com/faith /andy-stanley-responds-controversy-about-biblical-inerrancy/.

11 Grant R. Jeffrey, *Triumphant Return* (Colorado Springs: Waterbrook Press, 2001), p. 17.

12 Ray C. Stedman, *What on Earth Is Happening?* (Grand Rapids, Discovery House, 2003) pp. 120–121.

13 Got Questions website: https://www.gotquestions.org/fear-Lord-beginning-wisdom.html.

14 These points regarding Hebrew poetry come from a class on the Psalms I took at Talbot Seminary, which was taught by Richard Rigsby.

15 Homer A. Kent, Jr., *The Epistle to the Hebrews: a Commentary* (Grand Rapids: Baker Book House, 1972), p. 100.

16 Paul David Tripp, *New Morning Mercies* (Wheaton, IL: Crossway, 2014), August 26.

17 Dan B. Allender and Tremper Longman III, *The Cry of the Soul* (Colorado Springs, CO: NavPress, 1994), p. 102.

18 Ibid., p. 98.

19 Ibid., p. 99.

20 Ibid., p. 103.

21 Randy Alcorn, *Heaven* (Carol Stream, IL: Tyndale House, 2004), p. 52.

NOTES

22 Peter A. Steveson, *A Commentary on Proverbs* (Greenville, SC: Bob Jones University Press, 2001), p. 127.

23 Why is wisdom referred to as a she in Proverbs? Taken from the Got Questions website at https://www.gotquestions.org/wisdom-she-Proverbs.html.

24 D. Matthew Allen, , "Theology Adrift: The Early Church Fathers and Their Views of Eschatology," a paper published on the Bible.org website, chapter 5.

25 Ibid.

26 David Jeremiah, *Morning & Evening Devotions* (Nashville: Thomas Nelson, 2005), p. 304.

27 Jake Hibbs, *Living in the Daze of Deception* (Eugene, OR, Harvest House, 2024), p. 85.

28 D. Edmond Hiebert, *The Epistle of James* (Chicago: Moody Press, 1979), p. 228.

29 Ken Ham, "Biblical *Illiteracy Is at Astonishingly* High Levels in the Church, New Study Reveals," August 27, 2024 at: https://harbingersdaily.com/biblical-illiteracy-is-at-astonishingly-high-levels-in-the-church-new-study-reveals/.

30 Grant R. Jeffrey, *Triumphant Return*, (Colorado Springs: Waterbrook Press, 2001), p. 17.

31 Andrew M. Woods, *The Coming Kingdom* (Duluth, MN: Grace Gospel Press, 2016), p. 163.

32 Adam Eliyahu Berkowitz, "Ben Gurion Gearing up to Bring All 70 Nations Straight from the Airport to Third Temple," September 7, 2022 at https://www.israel365news.com/274549/ben-gurion-gearing-up-to-bring-all-70-nations-straight-from-the-airport-to-third-temple/.

33 Irenaeus, *Against Heresies, The Ante-Nicene Fathers*, 10 vols., Vol. 1 (Grand Rapids, MI: Eerdmans, 1979), p. 560.

34 Henry A. Ironside, *Expository Notes on the Epistles of James and Peter* (New York: Loizeaux Brothers, 1947), pp. 98–99.

35 Grant R. Jeffrey, *Triumphant Return: The Coming Kingdom of God* (Colorado Springs, CO: Waterbrook Press, 2001), p. 124.

36 Justin Martyr, "Dialogue with Trypho," *The Ante-Nicene Fathers,* 10 vols., Vol. 1 (Grand Rapids, MI: Eerdmans, 1979), pp. 239–40.

37 Paul David Tripp, "The Doctrine of Holiness," September 10, 2018, an article on his website: https://www.paultripp.com/articles/posts/the-doctrine-of-holiness-article

38 Erich Sauer, *The Triumph of the Crucified* (Eerdmans, Grand Rapids, MI, 1952), p. 150.

39 Ibid.

40 Tripp, *New Morning Mercies* August 14.

41 Ibid., January 5.

42 William C. Watson, *Dispensationalism Before Darby* (Navasota, TX, Lampion House, 2023), p. 73.

43 Ibid.

44 Ibid., pp. 74–75.

45 Ibid., p. 75.

46 Menasseh Ben Israel, *The Hope of Israel*, 2nd edition (London, 1652), translator's preface.

47 Wikipedia, *Menasseh Ben Israel*.

48 William Watson, "The Rise of Philo-Semitism and Premillennialism During the Seventeenth and Eighteenth Centuries," Pre-Tribulation Research Center website, https://www.pre-trib.org/articles/all-articles.

49 Jonathan C. Brentner, *The Triumph of the Redeemed* (Crane, MO: Defender, 2021), p. 89.

50 Ed Hindson, *Future Glory* (Eugene, OR: Harvest House, 2021), p. 129.

51 Martyr, "Dialogue with Trypho.".

52 Hibbs, *Living in the Daze of Deception*, p. 82.

53 Ibid.

54 Hindson, *Future Glory*, pp. 28–29.

55 Ibid, p. 29.

56 J. Dwight Pentecost, *Things to Come* (Grand Rapids: Zondervan, 1958), p. 248.

57 Lee W. Brainard, *Ten Potent Proofs for the Pretribulation Rapture* (Soothkeep Press, 2024) pp. 27–28.

58 Hindson, *Future Glory*, p. 14.

59 Ibid., p. 15.

60 Watson, *Dispensationalism Before Darby*, p. 137.

61 Ibid.

62 Ibid., p. 177.

63 Terry James and Jonathan C. Brentner, *Hereafter* (Crane, MO: Defender Publishing, 2024), p. 23.

64 Ibid.

65 Irenaeus, "Against Heresies," p. 558.

66 Cyprian, *Treatises of Cyprian*, "On the Mortality," section 25.

67 Rhodes, *Bible Prophecy under Siege*, p. 202.

68 Ibid.

69 Brentner, *Triumph of the Redeemed*, p. 107.

70 John MacArthur, *The MacArthur New Testament Commentary—1 & 2 Thessalonians* (Chicago: Moody Press, 2002), p. 136.

71 Brainard, *Ten Potent Proofs*, p. 38.

72 Ibid., pp. 38–39

73 Andy Woods, *The Falling Away—Spiritual Departure or Physical Rapture?* (Taos, NM: Dispensational Publishing House, 2018), p. 43.

74 D. Edmond Hiebert, *The Thessalonian Epistles* (Chicago: Moody Press, 1971), p. 301.

75 Ibid., p. 302.

76 Rhodes, *Bible Prophecy Under Siege*, p. 201.

77 Pentecost, *Things to Come*, p. 230.

78 Woods, *The Falling Away*, p. 16.

79 Brentner, *The Triumph of the Redeemed*, p. 147.

80 Woods, *The Falling Away*, p. 19.

81 Cyprian, *Treatises of Cyprian*, "On the Mortality," section 25.

82 Walvoord, *The Rapture Question*, p. 73.

83 Brainard, *Ten Potent Proofs*, p. 51.

84 Brentner, *Hereafter*, p. 38.

85 Brainard, *Ten Potent Proofs*, p. 45.

86 Ibid., p. 47.

87 Walvoord, *The Rapture Question*, p. 12.

88 Arnold Fruchtenbaum, *The Footsteps of the Messiah* (San Antonio: Ariel Ministries, 2021), p. 154.

NOTES

89 The apostle also used this same Greek word in John 11:29 about Mary: "And when she heard it, she rose quickly and went to him." It makes no sense to translate the verse as "she rose soon."

90 Pentecost, *Things to Come*, p. 208.

91 Fruchtenbaum, *Footsteps of the Messiah*, pp. 166–67.

92 Ibid, p. 166.

93 Fruchtenbaum, *Footsteps of the Messiah*, pp. 166–67.

94 John MacArthur, *The MacArthur New Testament Commentary—Revelation 1–11* (Chicago: Moody Press, 1999), p. 149.

95 Brainard, *Ten Potent Proofs*, p. 64.

96 Ed Hindson, *Future Glory*, p. 205.

97 Ray C. Stedman, *What on Earth Is Happening?* (Grand Rapids: Discovery House, 2003), pp. 146–47.

98 Ibid., p. 146.

99 Colin Brown, ed., *Dictionary of New Testament Theology Vol. 2*, (Grand Rapids, MI: Zondervan, 1969) p. 244.

100 Rhodes, *Bible Prophecy under Siege*, p. 208.

101 Wayne A. Brindle, "Imminence," *The Popular Encyclopedia of Bible Prophecy*, eds. Tim LaHaye and Ed Hindson (Eugene, OR: Harvest House, 2004), p. 145.

102 Brentner, *The Triumph of the Redeemed*, p. 164.

103 James and Brentner, *Hereafter*, pp. 35–38

104 Walvoord, *The Rapture Question*, p. 12.

105 Hindson, *Future Glory*, p. 150.

106 Watson, Is this from *Dispensationalism before Darby?* p. 137.

107 John Gill, as quoted in William Watson, *Dispensationalism before Darby*, p. 322.

108 Grant R. Jeffrey, *Triumphant Return: The Coming Kingdom of God* (Colorado Springs, CO: Waterbrook Press, 2001), p. 174.

109 Dr. David Reagan, *Six Reasons Why Every Christian Should Desire the Soon Return of Jesus*, September 13, 2024, article on the Harbinger's Daily website at: https://harbingersdaily .com/six-reasons-why-every-christian-should-desire-the-soon-return-of-jesus/.

www.ingramcontent.com/pod-product-compliance
Lightning Source LLC
Jackson TN
JSHW032105200425
82984JS00007B/22